BEAUTIFUL GARDENS

A VISITORS' GUIDE

Diane and Jon Sutherland (text) are professional writers, having written over 130 books since 1985. They are the authors of a wide variety of books, spanning children's reference, true crime, the paranormal, military history and education. They have won several literary prizes, including New York Libraries' Best of Reference and Booklist Editors Choice Award. They are both keen gardeners and have visited a large number of the gardens featured in this book.

Publisher & Creative Director: Nick Wells
Project Editor: Sarah Goulding
Designer: Mike Spender
Picture Researcher: Melinda Révèsz
Thanks to: Polly Willis

This is a **STAR FIRE** Book

STAR FIRE BOOKS
Crabtree Hall, Crabtree Lane
Fulham, London, SW6 6TY
United Kingdom

www.star-fire.co.uk

Star Fire is part of The Foundry Creative Media Company Limited

First published 2005

ISBN 1 84451 328 9

A copy of the CIP data for this book is available from the British Library.

Printed in China

BEAUTIFUL GARDENS

A VISITORS' GUIDE

WRITTEN BY JON & DIANE SUTHERLAND

STAR
FIRE

CONTENTS

CONTENTS

INTRODUCTION

Undoubtedly, British gardens existed in some form before the arrival of the Romans, but they certainly were the first really serious gardeners. They created the first courtyard gardens, complete with fountains and pools, and imported many plants and trees now common to this country.

The Middle Ages saw the monks as being the primary gardeners, concentrating on vegetables and herbs for medicines. By the time the Tudor period arrived, gardens had become great art and fashion. The royals and the rich demanded spectacular gardens and parks to complement their stately homes. They introduced knot gardens, hedge mazes and sundials and, above all, they began to bring plants and trees from the four corners of the earth.

By the 17th century, gardening in Britain was strongly influenced by the Dutch and the French. With William of Orange on the throne, the late 17th century saw Dutch water features, topiary and bulbs. By the 18th century the fashion was for informal gardens, and parkland was being incorporated into traditional gardens to provide breathtaking vistas.

This was the high point of the career of Lancelot Capability Brown. His basic design formula incorporated water, trees and terrain. He believed that all three should be moulded and he did this to great effect in countless locations around the country.

In direct contrast to Capability Brown's vision of moulding the landscape and bringing it in towards the house was the approach taken by Humphry Repton. He is, perhaps, as responsible as any for promoting the idea of a traditional garden, particularly flower gardens. It was a tradition that would extend well into the Victorian period with the Victorian love of follies, greenhouses, plants and, above all, flowers. It was at this time that the arboretum was created in order to house tree specimens from foreign shores.

The wild garden came into existence towards the end of the 19th century. William Robinson believed that the plant itself was the very heart of a garden. By the beginning of the last century wild gardens vied with traditional, formal gardens, and soon after Gertrude Jekyll developed what we

now recognise as being the herbaceous border.

The development continued as successive waves of fashion and design swept across the gardens of Britain. In any corner of the country you will discover gardens with roots dating back to the 15th century alongside gardens that have barely been established for 10 years. There are influences from every corner of the earth, both in terms of style, design and the plants chosen. The most unlikely combinations and most unpromising locations have been chosen by gardeners to make their mark on the landscape.

For hundreds of years the British have had a passion for gardening and visiting gardens is no new thing – it has been popular since the 17th century. There is, quite rightly, mass appeal for the innumerable landscape parks, gardens and pleasure grounds around the country.

The British garden is often thought to be naturalistic, but across the country you will see examples of artificial and formal styles, introduced from the late 17th century to the early 20th century. Many of the gardens have the three requisite elements of a truly British garden: an ornamental garden, a wild garden and a walled garden. These three basic elements were subject to constant changes and taste in fashion, although fortuitously some of those that had been swept away by time and other tastes have since been restored.

In order to enjoy the parks and gardens all the more, it is useful to understand the period in which they were made. Many of the grand gardens were a reflection of the owner's social standing and power, and they were often keen for garden designers such as Capability Brown to transform the landscape, showing their control over nature. Many of the schemes were highly controversial at the time, not to mention expensive and ambitious. Rivers were forced to change their course, areas were flooded, hillsides stripped and flattened and woodlands planted to conceal the house and garden and provide an artificial vista for the occupants.

Understanding historical gardens does not only need an understanding of plants and trees, but even archaeology. Many gardeners have painstakingly reconstructed gardens from the flimsiest of evidence, to recreate knot gardens, medieval vegetable plots and a host of other long-lost garden features.

interesting, there are gardens to excite, captivate, inspire and bring emotion.

British gardens have enjoyed popularity for several centuries and quietly they have gone about their work, surviving the seasons, developing, expanding and bringing joy. The more recent popularity for gardening on television has brought a boom time to the gardens, whether they are ancient or modern. In every county there are gems that sparkle and gardens to marvel at.

Whether your taste is for contrived garden design or for real or created wild nature, Britain provides something for everyone. In the most unexpected places you will find picturesque gardens, which would lead you to believe that you were in France, Holland, Italy, China, or even Japan. With significant contributions made by not just garden designers but individuals such as Sir Walter Scott and William Morris, Britain's gardens cannot help but be as diverse as possible. Systematically, landscaping has been undertaken, woodlands planted, terraces built, conservatories erected, rockeries formed and everywhere plants have been manipulated. The gardener contrives to create new shapes through topiary and bonsai, to fool the eye with lawns, statues and ruins. Everywhere there is colour, whether sprinklings of shades or carpet bedding. It is impossible to summarise British gardens and impossible to compare landscape as different as, for example, Chatsworth and Castle Howard.

It always seems that Britain is a country in bloom. In the spring daffodils, crocuses, hyacinths and tulips come alive, pushing through the damp and cold soil. Then it is the turn of the bedding plants, wallflowers, herbaceous borders, and alpines and, of course, the trees. The woodlands are carpeted

Although there are grand, huge and extravagant landscaped gardens contained in this book, there are others that are more modest, but no less important. Across the centuries, gardeners, within the limits of their funds and skills, have sought to create the widest variety of gardens in Britain. In Scotland, against the elements and the unpromising soil and conditions, fascinating gardens with sub-tropical plants have flourished. In Wales, the most mountainous part of the country, there are hidden oases such as Bodnant and Erddig. In the southwest of England, blessed with slightly more favourable weather conditions, there are plants from the southern hemisphere and the most astonishing and largest greenhouses in the world at the Eden Project. Across the length and breadth of Britain, often hidden, sometimes neglected, but always loved and with bluebells and primroses. By summer, fields of crops are dotted with bright red poppies, roses are coming into bloom and the air is full of the scent of honeysuckle and jasmine. By the late summer the eye is drawn to chrysanthemums, geraniums, fuchsias, begonias and dahlias. In Norfolk and in other places the lavender is ready to harvest, while butterflies and bees flit around herb gardens and the orchards are laden with fruit. The vintners are preparing to harvest their grapes and everywhere there are fresh, thriving vegetables. When autumn turns to winter there are pansies to provide colour along with aconites and anemones. Snowdrops provide drifts of stark colour amongst the trees and the holly and mistletoe are almost ready for Christmas.

This book celebrates the sheer variety, scale, ingenuity, genius and persistence of generations of gardeners. Some are professionals; for some it was their life's work, whilst others have adapted fashionable themes and styles and learned all they know from the great masters.

Whether you are in the extreme southwest of England in a city, the wilds of Scotland or Northumbria, or indeed by any coast, you will find a garden, a tranquil place to admire. It may have been the labour of many centuries and several generations of gardeners will have lovingly tendered the plants and trees and, over time, constructed the tapestry before your eyes. There are grand, outrageous and bizarre structures, which melt into the landscape of the gardens,

whether they be glasshouses, fountains, gazebos, temples, follies, old quarries, ruins or extravagant terraces. Whether your interest is in these structures or in herbaceous borders, woodlands, knot gardens, lawns, parterres, herbs, fountains, spring flowers, roses, walled gardens, follies, topiary, wild flowers, rockeries or strange, exotic and rare species of plant, they are all out there waiting for you to discover them.

A garden is not so much judged by its size and scope, but by its very wholeness and the way in which every detail complements all parts of it. The 150 gardens featured in this book are shown at their very best. The pictures reveal the labours of love, the attention to detail and the exquisite colour schemes, textures and general layout.

A British garden is so much more than the sum of its parts. It is not merely plants and trees, hard landscaping or a natural environment. All these British gardens open a window to inspiration and acclaim.

NORTHWEST of ENGLAND

Eleven gardens from Cheshire, Lancashire and Cumbria have been chosen to represent the huge variety of different gardens in this area. Many of this wide variety of gardens have been built around old halls or castles.

There is a wealth of history and heritage in the idyllic market towns and villages in this part of the country. This sense of history is reflected in its gardens. Cobble Hay, for example, has been a working farm for over 150 years and Brantwood Gardens are linked to the famous painter, critic and author, John Ruskin.

There are large and small gardens, formal gardens, landscaped terrain and a diverse range of themed and specialised gardens. Levens Hall has one of the oldest topiary gardens in Britain, whilst equally as stunning is the limestone rock garden created at Sizergh Castle in 1926.

In the northwest there are gardens that have been designed for both leisure and pleasure. Others are intriguing, such as the knot garden at Little Moreton Hall. Still others were expected to give a return to their owners or at least provide sufficient vegetables for the kitchens.

With plants from the Himalayas and Japan vying with daffodils and rhododendrons, this is a region of true variety.

 CUMBRIA

LEVENS HALL GARDEN

KENDAL, CUMBRIA

The garden is 5 miles to the south of Kendal on the A6.

Arguably this is the finest topiary garden in Britain and
was designed and planted in 1690. The magnificent avenue
of oak trees was saved from road builders in 1970 when the
area was zoned for the M6.

Beneath the topiary are bedding plants, but other parts
of the garden have equal appeal. Elsewhere you will find a
nuttery, rose garden and good herbaceous borders. The
latest addition, to celebrate 300 years, is a fountain garden
with pleached limes.

CORBY CASTLE

GREAT CORBY, CUMBRIA

The castle is on the east bank of the River Eden, 6 miles east of Carlisle on the A69.

Corby Castle was originally a 14th century tower house, which then belonged to the Salkeld family. The Howard family purchased the estate in the 17th century and added a wing to the building. By the 19th century, the tower and wing had been absorbed into a splendid mansion. The castle has outstanding landscaped gardens dating to the 18th century and is set on exceptional woodland riverside, on the banks of the River Eden. The woodlands boast a huge variety of trees.

HOLEHIRD GARDEN

PATTERDALE ROAD, WINDERMERE, CUMBRIA

The garden is half a mile to the north of Windermere, or one mile from Townend, on the A592.

The former owner of Holehird, William Groves, sponsored plant-collecting expeditions to the Himalayas. Unsurprisingly, Holehird, which is now run by a horticultural society, has both a stream and a woodland garden. Spring sees a stunning display of daffodils, but in late spring the magnolias, rhododendrons and azaleas steel the show. In the summer it is the turn of the walled garden, herbaceous borders and island beds. The National Collection of astilbes and hydrangeas dazzle visitors through late summer and into the autumn.

BRANTWOOD GARDEN

CONISTON, CUMBRIA

The garden is to the east of Coniston Water, off the B5285.

Between 1872 and 1900, John Ruskin, the painter, author and critic, lived at Brantwood. Using the ancient woodlands as inspiration, he developed several themes and added many exotic plant species.

The fern garden alone contains more than 250 native species and the moorland garden has two reservoirs, as well as naturalistic terraces. The latest addition to the garden, which is based on 130-year-old sketches by Ruskin, is the Zig-Zaggy. It allows visitors to travel through the garden.

HOLKER HALL AND GARDENS

CARK-IN-CARTMEL, GRANGE-OVER-SANDS, CUMBRIA

The gardens are 5 miles to the west of Grange-over-Sands on the B5277.

The centrepiece of this immaculately kept garden is the 25-acre woodland and formal gardens, which are nestled in the 200-acre site of parkland.

In the early 19th century, terraces, a conservatory, an arboretum and a large, walled kitchen garden were added. The delightful red sandstone hall is perfectly complemented by the colourful formal gardens, which still evolve with the old croquet lawn now planted as a garden room. The gardens represent an ever-changing environment, which will always intrigue.

THE ROCK GARDEN

SIZERGH CASTLE, KENDAL, CUMBRIA

The castle and gardens are 3.5 miles south of Kendal, northwest of the A590.

Although this old castle has a stunning lake and woodland garden, it is best known for its very large limestone rock garden, which T. R. Hayes & Sons created in 1926.

The rocky streams and pools are home to moisture loving plants and the National Collection of hardy ferns. Surrounding the castle are several specimen trees, formal terraces, herbaceous borders, a wild flower meadow and a Dutch garden. Around the castle itself you will also find roses and wall plants.

*L*ANCASHIRE

COBBLE HEY FARM AND GARDENS

OFF HOBB LANE, CLAUGHTON ON BROCK, GARSTANG, NEAR PRESTON, LANCASHIRE

The gardens are on the opposite side of the M6 to Garstang.

Cobble Hey has been a working farm for over 150 years, with marvellous views over the Forest of Bowland. The gardens have been open to the public since 2002. Cobble Hey boasts several cottage gardens, a seaside themed area and a wonderful mature woodland with wild flowers, ferns, spring-fed ponds and streams. Other stunning areas include a conifer bed, clipped box hedging and a rockery of alpines. In all, the gardens boast interest no matter what the season.

RUFFORD OLD HALL

RUFFORD, NEAR ORMSKIRK, LANCASHIRE

The hall and gardens are 7 miles north of Ormskirk.

The origins of the hall date back to the 1450s, but the building as it now appears probably dates to the 16th century and the then owner of the estate, Robert Hesketh.

The estate was presented to the National Trust in 1936, and is surrounded by Victorian-style gardens. The woodland areas have magnificent rhododendrons and azaleas, as well as topiary. There is an orchard with several varieties of apples, colourful herbaceous borders, climbing plants and several old fashioned plants.

GRESGARTH HALL

CATON, LANCASHIRE

From junction 34 of the M6 follow the signs to Kirby Lonsdale, then Caton.

The renowned garden designer, Arabella Lennox-Boyd, created these delightful gardens. The gardens cover 15 acres, including a lake, terraces, a bog garden, wild garden, a large kitchen garden and a bluebell wood.

The gardens have a stunning rhododendron hillside, a millennium wood, extensive herbaceous borders and a serpentine walk. Placed amongst the plants, trees and shrubs are several modern and classical sculptures. The gardens are well known for moisture-loving plants, including ferns, acers, lilacs, azaleas and magnolias.

CHESHIRE

KNOT GARDEN

LITTLE MORETON HALL, CONGLETON, CHESHIRE

The garden is 4 miles southwest of Congleton, east of the A34.

Little Moreton Hall, now bowed and misshapen by age, is a delightful hotchpotch of buildings and a central courtyard. The hall is probably Britain's most famous timber-framed manor house, the imposing black and white structure having been begun in 1450. When the National Trust took over the buildings and grounds, they commissioned the creation of a Knot Garden based on designs from 1670. The Knot Garden has geometric and symmetrical patterns picked out by evergreen herbs, which are planted in continuous ribbons.

TATTON PARK HOUSE

TATTON PARK, KNUTSFORD, CHESHIRE

The house is 2.5 miles north of Knutsford and is signposted from the M56 and M6.

Tatton Park is renowned for its diverse and themed gardens. They were inspired by several generations of the Egerton family and given to the National Trust in 1958, being maintained by Cheshire County Council.

Originally the estate spread over 25,000 acres, but now less than a tenth remains. Tatton Park has delightful early formal gardens, splendid topiary and rose gardens and an extensive range of walled kitchen gardens. There is also a wonderful terraced garden, a fern garden and Japanese garden.

Northeast of England

This is a region of the country encompassing Northumberland, Durham and Yorkshire. Whilst it boasts no less than four national parks (the Peak District, the Yorkshire Dales, the North York Moors and the Northumberland National Park), it also has a wonderful range of manmade landscapes.

Once again the hand of Capability Brown can be seen at Harewood House Garden and at Wallington Hall Garden. This was Capability Brown's birthplace and home as a child. Raby Castle, a dramatic 14th century structure, is set in 18th century gardens, whilst Herterton House Gardens date back to just 1976. The Bowes Museum is a French-style chateau surrounded by 20 acres of exciting plants and trees. Studley Royal's gardens were created at the beginning of the 18th century and as if a canal, moon ponds and a temple were not enough, the garden also boasts the ruins of Fountains Abbey. At Burnby Hall there is a collection inspired by a military man, obsessed with water lilies. Of equal importance are the environmentally friendly gardens, extending to 12 acres, at Long Framlington.

The gardens of the northeast of England have much to offer – from a Victorian peach house and a walled garden with heated flues, to a grand parterre, Edwardian glasshouses and walled gardens enough to whet the appetite of any garden enthusiast.

NORTHUMBERLAND

BELSAY HALL GARDEN

BELSAY, NEAR PONTELAND, NEWCASTLE-UPON-TYNE, NORTHUMBERLAND

The gardens are 7 miles to the northwest of Ponteland.

The stones for Sir Charles Monck's 14th century castle, which is a Neo-classic house, were taken from a quarry within the grounds. The quarry was then transformed into a picturesque gorge. Although some of the gardens date to the late 1700s, the majority can be traced to the 19th century. The terraces that surround the house overlook a magnificent rhododendron garden. The terraces themselves have wonderful bedding displays and herbaceous borders. There are also woodland walks around the lake.

WALLINGTON HALL GARDEN

CAMBO, MORPETH, NORTHUMBERLAND

The gardens are on the B6343, 12 miles to the west of Morpeth.

Wallington Hall itself is 17th century, whilst the park and gardens date from the 18th century. The gravel terrace that overlooks the pond and lawn was built in the 1730s. Capability Brown lived in the neighbourhood as a child and in 1765 helped design the East Garden and the China Pond. The landscape is formal but natural and extends out to the moor. The walled garden has many beautiful climbers and magnificent borders. There is a Victorian peach house and Edwardian conservatory in the grounds.

HERTERTON HOUSE GARDENS

HATRINGTON, CAMBO, MORPETH, NORTHUMBERLAND

The gardens are 12 miles to the west of Morpeth, on the B6342.

This 16th century farmhouse is surrounded by gardens created since 1976 by Frank and Marjorie Lawley. There are four distinctive areas of the garden: the winter garden, the flower garden, the knot garden and the fancy garden. The flower garden, shown here, is the main feature and is romantic and informal. The knot garden contains a wide selection of traditional medicinal herbs. The owners have chosen to use many unusual, traditional plants, including wild species, which all flourish in these gardens.

LONGFRAMLINGTON GARDENS

SWARLAND ROAD, LONGFRAMLINGTON, MORPETH, NORTHUMBERLAND

The gardens are off the A697, a short distance along the B6345.

This 12-acre site boasts thousands of different trees, shrubs, perennials, climbers, herbs and rock garden plants. The gardens are designed to have an environmentally friendly impact and provide scientific information to lower carbon dioxide emissions and encourage the conservation of natural biodiversity. The 'Living Exhibition of Plants' provides an integrated design over the garden, which was started in 1998. The plant collection now extends to 2,500 species, including some unusual specimens.

DURHAM

BOWES MUSEUM GARDEN

BOWES MUSEUM, BARNARD CASTLE, DURHAM

The garden is situated to the southeast of Barnard Castle.

This French-style chateau was designed in 1869, with the gardens laid out in 1981 in order to complement the style of the building. There are 20 acres of grounds, with 56 different species of trees. A double avenue circles the park. Beneath the stone balustrade of the building is a traditional herbaceous border and a formal parterre. The raised beds of the parterre are edged with box and if laid out in a line, would extend to 1.5 miles.

RABY CASTLE GARDENS

STAINDROP, DARLINGTON, DURHAM

The gardens are one mile to the north of Staindrop.

This highly dramatic, 14th century castle has the appearance of a Gothic folly, set in a deer park and gardens. The deer park, extending to 200 acres, has red, black, mottled and fallow deer. The gardens are traditional 18th century, designed by Thomas Wright. The walled garden, with heated flues, allows sub-tropical fruits to be grown. There is a fig planted in 1786 which still fruits annually. There are rose gardens, formal lawns and a beautiful heather and conifer garden.

YORKSHIRE

HAREWOOD HOUSE GARDEN

HAREWOOD, LEEDS, YORKSHIRE

The gardens are 7 miles to the north of Leeds and 7 miles south of Harrogate, on the A61.

Harewood House was begun in 1758 and the park, designed by Capability Brown, completed between 1758 and 1772. Later Charles Barry created a great terrace to act as a transition point between the house and the park. The terrace has a grand parterre and beyond that a walled garden, a rose garden and an oriental garden. The spring daffodils are magnificent, as are the enormous numbers of rhododendrons. The gardens have been much praised and painted by both J. M. W. Turner and Thomas Girtin.

STUDLEY ROYAL
AND FOUNTAINS ABBEY
RIPON, YORKSHIRE

The gardens are 4 miles west of Ripon, off the B6265.

The original work on the gardens at Studley Royal took place between 1718 and 1742, under the direction of the then owner, John Aislabie. The gardens have a canal and moon ponds, overlooked by the Temple of Piety, which was completed in 1730. The former water garden is rather like a water parterre, one of which can be seen at Chantilly. The gardens are set in a wooded valley, dotted with temples and statues. Beyond that are the ruins of Fountains Abbey, destroyed in the Reformation by Henry VIII.

CASTLE HOWARD
GARDEN
YORK, YORKSHIRE

The gardens are 15 miles to the northeast of York.

Work began on the palace in 1701, placing it rather theatrically on a natural ridge. The grand avenue was then begun and the classical landscape was created. Later, in the 19th century, W. A. Nesfield designed new gardens. There are extensive walks along terraces through formal gardens and woodlands. The Boar Garden alone has thousands of daffodils and spring bulbs, notably the crocuses, snowdrops and tulips. The herbaceous borders, roses and rhododendrons provide spectacular changes of colour throughout the year.

BURNBY HALL GARDENS

NEAR POCKLINGTON, YORKSHIRE

The gardens are near the market town of Pocklington, just off the A1079.

Major Percy Stewart, an adventurer and traveller that went round the world seven times, created these gardens. He gave up hunting and became obsessed with water lilies. It is therefore no surprise that the gardens hold the National Collection of hardy water lilies, with over 100 varieties. The gardens extend to some eight acres and are designed to show the lilies in their natural settings. There are upper and lower lakes, together with ornamental trees, shrubs, flowers and plants.

EAST of ENGLAND

The east of England is renowned as the area that produces at least three very distinctive forms of popular English flowers. For many years Cambridgeshire, and particularly the market town of Wisbech, has been the main rose growing area of the country. Whilst Norfolk, at least since the Victorian period, has been the home of English lavender, north Norfolk, often referred to as 'poppy land', has fields ablaze with poppies during harvest time.

The east of England encompasses Lincolnshire, Leicestershire, Nottinghamshire, Northamptonshire, Cambridgeshire, Norfolk and Suffolk and within this vast area there are gardens to intrigue and to delight. From the 1,000-acre Belton House near Grantham in Lincolnshire to the smaller but just as delightful Hodstock Priory Gardens near Worksop, there is history, endeavour and inspiration.

There are royal gardens at Sandringham, monastic connections at Anglesey Abbey, and the former home of *Gardener's World* at Barnsdale Gardens in Rutland. There are gardens that have been tended for decades by successive generations and others, such as Easton walled gardens, which lay dormant and abandoned for half a century. From the grandeur and history of Ickworth and Somerleyton, there are newer, but no less grand, new gardens, such as those at Pensthorpe near Fakenham.

LINCOLNSHIRE

BELTON HOUSE PARK AND GARDENS

GRANTHAM, LINCOLNSHIRE

The house and gardens are 3 miles north of Grantham, off the A607.

The French-style house dates to 1688 and the gardens, which were strongly influenced by Capability Brown, were designed by William Emes and feature a canal and temple. The grounds are extensive with 1,000 acres given over to woodland walks, lakes and avenues. The conservatory and formal garden both date back to 1811. The Dutch Garden, with an orangery and statue walk, was created in the 1870s. The sunken Italian Garden, created by Jeffry Wyattvile, was built at the beginning of the 19th century.

DODDINGTON HALL GARDEN

LINCOLN, LINCOLNSHIRE

The gardens are 5 miles to the west of Lincoln, on the B1190.

Robert Smythson, who incorporated a walled garden and gatehouse, designed Doddington Hall in 1600. The five acre walled gardens have a knot garden, fountains and magnificent borders featuring the flag iris. Spring sees flowering shrubs and bulbs, particularly snowdrops, followed by dog-toothed violets, lilies and roses. Later in the year there are wonderful winter flowering rhododendrons and witch hazel. All of these perfectly complement old trees, water gardens, a temple of the winds and a turf maze.

EASTON WALLED GARDENS

EASTON, GRANTHAM, LINCOLNSHIRE

The gardens are on the A1, between Grantham and Stamford.

Henry Cholmeley bought the Easton manor in 1592, which included gardens, meadows and orchards. Unfortunately the house was demolished in the 1950s, but the walled gardens, extending to 12 acres, still remain. For 50 years the site was left abandoned, but in 2000 work began to restore the garden. You can now see mature lime tree avenues, cedars of Lebanon, Wellingtonia and yew and box hedges. Recent discoveries include unusual snowdrops, rare lilacs and laburnums, all within hundreds of yards of walling.

GRIMSTHORPE CASTLE AND PARK

GRIMSTHORPE, BOURNE, LINCOLNSHIRE

The gardens are 4 miles northwest of Bourne, on the A151.

Grimsthorpe has been the home of the Eresby family since 1516. Sir John Vanbrugh designed the manor house and Capability Brown designed the park in 1771. The grounds have a knot garden, hedged rose gardens and a terrace with shrub and herbaceous borders. Peter Coates and the Countess of Ancaster created the ornamental vegetable garden and orchard in the 1960s. The gardens flow beautifully from the formal gardens, through topiary and into lake views from the woodlands.

UTLAND

BARNSDALE GARDENS

THE AVENUE, EXTON,
OAKHAM, RUTLAND

Between Stamford and Oakham on the A606.

The gardens, centred around a Victorian house, were designed by the late television gardener Geoff Hamilton. Work began in 1984 and the five acres became the home of *Gardener's World*. There are no less than 30 distinct areas in the gardens, ranging from a stream and bog garden, through to an Elizabethan vegetable garden. Geoff was working on the Town Paradise Garden in June 1995 when he suffered his first heart attack and his last work can be seen in the Reclaim Garden.

$\mathcal{N}$OTTINGHAMSHIRE

HODSTOCK PRIORY GARDENS

BLYTH, NEAR WORKSOP, NOTTINGHAMSHIRE

The gardens are 16 miles east of Sheffield and 1 mile southwest of Blyth.

Hodstock Priory was listed in the Domesday Book. Its gatehouse dates to 1500, but the house and gardens are Victorian. The gardens have a terrace, herbaceous borders, a bog garden, an old moat and a lake. To celebrate the millennium, 250,000 snowdrops were planted to add to the already impressive display, which takes you through a half-mile carpeted walk. There is a myriad of flowers and plants over the five acre site, boasting aconites, hellebores and cyclamen.

NEWSTEAD ABBEY GARDEN

NEWSTEAD ABBEY PARK, LINBY, RAVENSHEAD, NOTTINGHAMSHIRE

The gardens are 12 miles north of Nottingham and 1 mile west of the A60.

Lord Byron once owned this former Augustinian abbey. It has expansive gardens, incorporating lawns, a medieval garden, a lake, a rock garden and the renowned Japanese Garden. The Japanese Garden, shown here, was created in about 1900 and is recognised as probably the first of its type in Britain. Most of the other gardens date to the 19th century (between 1861 and 1900). The recently restored long border, which is 220 metres (720 feet) in length, provides a magnificent display throughout the summer months.

THORESBY HALL

NEAR OLLERTON, NEWARK, NOTTINGHAMSHIRE

The gardens are between junctions 29 and 30 of the M1.

This Grade 1 listed Victorian building, now a hotel, sits in a 65-acre site with a circumference of 12 miles. The trees, including silver birch, were planted over 100 years ago. There are graceful beeches and Spanish chestnuts dotted around the undulating terrain. Huge numbers of ferns, which transform from green to golden and then reddish brown, cover the ground. A shallow stream cascades down a waterfall and a broad, clear lake extends as far as the eye can see.

 EICESTERSHIRE

WHATTON GARDENS

WHATTON ESTATE, LONG WHATTON, LOUGHBOROUGH, LEICESTERSHIRE

The gardens are off the A6, between Hathern and Kegworth.

The gardens at Whatton cover some 25 acres, packed with trees, shrubs and rock pools. The 40 acre parkland was developed in the 19th century and there are an additional five acres of formal, oriental and ornamental gardens. The gardens were further developed and restored during the middle of the last century. The estate gardens, owned by Lord and Lady Crawshaw, date back to 1802 and have shrub and herbaceous borders, lawn, rose and wild gardens, pools, an arboretum, mature trees and spring bulbs.

THE MANOR HOUSE

MANOR ROAD, DONINGTON-LE-HEATH, COALVILLE, LEICESTERSHIRE

The gardens are on the outskirts of Coalville, between Donington-le-Heath and Hugglescote.

These gardens are reconstructed versions of primarily 17th century styles, surrounding a 13th century stone house. The flower garden was created using contemporary books along with plants shown in a catalogue dated 1607. The herb garden incorporates medieval plants used for remedies for diseases and illnesses of the period, while the ornamental maze is a development of the Elizabethan knot garden. The orchard, planted in 2000, includes apples, pear, quince, medlar, gage, plums and filberts. The plant and tree varieties provide habitats for wildlife.

*N*ORTHAMPTONSHIRE

KIRBY HALL

NEAR CORBY, NORTHAMPTONSHIRE

The gardens are off the A43, 4 miles to the northeast of Corby.

The impressive, understated shell of Kirby Hall dates back to 1570. In the mid-19th century the owner was forced to demolish much of the building to pay gambling debts. The house and gardens are now in the hands of English Heritage, who are gradually refitting the house and restoring the gardens. The gardens have been recreated using the original 17th century designs, boasting fine topiary and distinctively elaborate cutwork. Gradually, the decorative carvings and ornate gardens are being restored to their former glory.

COTTESBROOKE HALL GARDEN

COTTESBROOKE, NORTHAMPTONSHIRE

The gardens are 10 miles north of Northampton, between the A508 and the A5119.

Enclosed courtyards with urns and statues, a wild garden and a woodland garden surround this fine Queen Anne house which dates to 1702. The gardens boast wonderful 18th century landscaping, providing great, sweeping views down to the lakes. A number of distinguished landscape designers have been involved in the project, including Sir Geoffrey Jellicoe and Dame Sylvia Crowe. They, amongst others, have been responsible for the formal and wild gardens that surround the house, the main inspiration coming from the late Lady MacDonald-Buchan.

LAMPORT HALL AND GARDENS

LAMPORT, NORTHAMPTONSHIRE

The gardens are 8 miles north of Northampton, on the A508.

Surrounded by a huge park and tranquil gardens is Lamport Hall, which was begun in 1655. The gardens were started in the same year, under the guidance of Gilbert Clarke. Only the surrounding bank and wrought iron gates remain. The sycamores and cedars date to the 1820s, planted by Mary Isham, who also planned the planting of the parkland. There is a 24 foot alpine garden, probably the oldest in Britain, along with an Italian garden and rockery.

 CAMBRIDGESHIRE

ANGLESEY ABBEY GARDENS

ANGLESEY ABBEY, LODE, CAMBRIDGESHIRE

The gardens are 6 miles northeast of Cambridge, in the village of Lode.

The gardens here were developed in 1926 by the first Lord Fairhaven and are built around an Augustan priory. The gardens are best described as being in a mixed style. They have a monks garden, daffodil walk, herbaceous garden, arboretum, a temple lawn and a water mill. There are majestic tree-lined avenues, giving way to secluded formal gardens featuring dahlias, snowdrops and herbaceous plants. Throughout the gardens are examples of Lord Fairhaven's collection of statuary, which complement the garden designs.

ELTON HALL GARDEN

NEAR PETERBOROUGH, CAMBRIDGESHIRE

The gardens are 8 miles to the west of Peterborough, in the village of Elton.

Elton Hall itself was completed in 1666, but the beautiful gardens themselves date back to the 15th century. The grounds include a rose garden, lily pond and herbaceous borders. The original Victorian gardens have now been fully restored and include a knot garden, a Gothic style orangery and a fascinating collection of trees. The gardens are well known for their old-fashioned roses, colourful herbaceous borders and well-maintained hedges.

PECKOVER HOUSE AND GARDENS

NORTH BRINK, WISBECH, CAMBRIDGESHIRE

The gardens are in Wisbech on the north bank of the River Nene.

A Quaker banking family owned this Georgian house, but the gardens are distinctly Victorian in nature. The gardens have wonderful old trees, conservatories, herbaceous borders designed by Graham Stuart Thomas, summerhouses and walled enclosures. Specimen trees, such as chuson palms, tulip trees, monkey puzzles and gingko, surround the expansive lawns. The orangery has colourful pot plants and fruit trees. In addition there are magnificent roses, a Victorian fernery and ribbon borders, something for any time of the year.

WIMPOLE HALL GARDEN

ARRINGTON, ROYSTON, CAMBRIDGESHIRE

The garden is off the A60, 7 miles southwest of Cambridge.

Wimpole Hall Garden has many influences, from London and Wise, through Charles Bridgeman to Capability Brown. It was Brown that transformed the gardens into a serpentine park with three lakes and a belt of trees. The National Trust reinstated the formal parterre in the shape of a Union Jack. The gardens hold the National Collection of walnut trees. The spring sees narcissus and daffodils, followed by tulips amongst the woodland garden and trails. Not to be missed is the Chinese Bridge.

~~NORFOLK~~

BLICKLING HALL GARDEN

AYLSHAM, NORFOLK

The garden is 1.5 miles northwest of Aylsham, on the B1354.

Blickling Hall dates to 1611 and the woodland wilderness to 1629. The gardens were shown on an estate map dated 1729, revealing radiating avenues extending from the enclosed garden near to the house. W. A. Nesfield and Sir Digby Wyat designed the formal Victorian garden in 1872 and Norah Lindsey simplified it in the 1930s. The gardens are worth visiting all year round, with spring bulbs, azaleas, herbaceous borders, rhododendrons and a flower parterre. The temple, orangery and yew topiary should not be missed.

SANDRINGHAM HOUSE GARDEN

SANDRINGHAM, KING'S LYNN, NORFOLK

The gardens are 8 miles northeast of King's Lynn, on the B1440.

The house, built in 1902, is the Queen's country retreat. It has expansive lawns, woodland gardens, two lakes, a huge rock garden and a hedge-enclosed garden that was designed by Sir Geoffrey Jellicoe in 1947. Jellicoe was also responsible for the herbaceous borders. The gardens have magnificent woodlands with many fine trees and are renowned for their magnolias, camellias and rhododendrons. The house has seen four generations of monarchs and is described as the most comfortable house in England.

HOLKHAM HALL AND NURSERY GARDENS

WELLS-NEXT-THE-SEA, NORFOLK

The gardens are 2 miles to the west of Wells-next-the-Sea and 35 miles northwest of Norwich.

This 18th century house and deer park has some original features, but the gardens are largely Victorian in style. The arch and obelisk were built in the 1730s and the lake by Capability Brown in 1762. W. A. Nesfield designed the terraced garden in 1854. The nursery gardens, famed for their elegant design and glasshouses, include a vinery and a carnation house. In all they cover six acres, and contain everything from shrubs to climbers and roses to herbs.

PENSTHORPE

FAKENHAM, NORFOLK

The gardens are a mile from Fakenham, on the A1067.

Pensthorpe is a millennium garden, opened in 2000 and designed by Piet Oudolf. The gardens are famed for their naturalist planting, with deep borders of grasses and perennials in drifts of colour and texture. Most striking is the fact that the plants are English herbaceous border varieties, used in a radically different way. In 2005, the Wave Garden, designed by Julie Toll, was opened. Her design blends naturalistic looks with formal touches. It is primarily designed as a spring and early summer garden.

SUFFOLK

ICKWORTH HOUSE
AND PARK

HORRINGER, BURY ST EDMONDS, SUFFOLK

The gardens are 3 miles to the southwest of Bury St Edmonds, off the A143.

Ickworth House was built between 1794 and 1830 and set in a park designed by Capability Brown. The Italian garden, however, with its specimen trees and hedging, is Victorian. The park contains some of the best ancient examples of oak, beech and hornbeam trees. The Silver Garden has stones from Ireland's Giant's Causeway and a Victorian stumpery. In addition to the many woodland walks is a particularly fine orangery, boasting lemon trees. The National Trust now tends the house and gardens.

ABBEY GARDENS
ANGEL HILL, BURY ST EDMONDS, SUFFOLK

The gardens are in the heart of Bury St Edmonds.

These former botanical gardens are set alongside the River Lark. The gardens have award winning flower displays and include the Appleby Rose Garden and the Pilgrim's Herb Garden. The gardens are framed by the abbey wall, which extends from the Abbot's Bridge to St Edmundsbury Cathedral. The largest garden is a huge circle of flowerbeds, which are surrounded by lawns. More secluded gardens to view include the water garden and the blind garden, which is rich in scent.

SOMERLEYTON HALL AND GARDENS
NEAR LOWESTOFT, SUFFOLK

The gardens are 5 miles northwest of Lowestoft.

Somerleyton Hall was made for a wealthy contractor who built the Houses of Parliament. W. A. Nesfield redesigned the gardens, which have a yew hedge dating to 1846, scores of specimen evergreen trees, parterres and glasshouses designed by Joseph Paxton. The gardens are also notable for John Thomas's garden sculptures. In spring the gardens have colourful rhododendrons and azaleas. The walled garden, with its collection of small trees, is ablaze with under-planted daffodils and a huge variety of climbers.

HEART of ENGLAND

As you would expect from an area that straddles the centre of England, there is almost unrivalled countryside, history and heritage to be found in the heart of England. There are a vast number of stately homes, castles and, of course, gardens.

The heart of England encompasses the countryside of Derbyshire, Staffordshire, Shropshire, Warwickshire, Worcestershire, Herefordshire, Gloucestershire and Oxfordshire and the more urban West Midlands. As an area at the heart of international trade and industry through the centuries, there are enormous influences from Italy, Holland, China, Egypt, Switzerland and France. The styles of garden range from the Elizabethan to the Arts and Crafts by way of the Edwardians and the Victorians.

In the heart of England you will find Georgian houses cheek by jowl with Victorian gardens and medieval castles with 16th and 17th century garden designs. As in many parts of the country, the imprint of Capability Brown can be found, such as at Charlecote near Warwick, where he has shaped the landscape to give it an even more naturalistic effect. Other important figures include Charles Bridgeman, Heather Muir and the influence of William Morris.

A particular high point is Blenheim Palace Garden, a vast estate transformed by Capability Brown and boasting the arboretum in which Winston Churchill proposed to his 'dear Clementine'.

ERBYSHIRE

CHATSWORTH GARDEN

BAKEWELL, DERBYSHIRE

The gardens are off the B6012, 3 miles to the east of Bakewell.

Chatsworth House was created in the 17th century and since then there have been several additions and modifications. The gardens are 19th century and the park 18th century. Capability Brown was involved in the design, altering the course of the River Derwent and removing many of the old formal gardens. In the 19th century Sir Joseph Paxton created a mixed style garden close to the house and added parterre gardens. There is also a rock garden, lakes, kitchen garden, a maze and fountains.

HADDON HALL GARDEN

BAKEWELL, DERBYSHIRE

The gardens are 1.5 miles to the south of Bakewell, on the A6.

The house is essentially a medieval castle with 17th century-style gardens, which are an English version of a 16th century Italian garden. The 9th Duchess of Rutland created most of what can be seen at the beginning of the 20th century. The gardens were overgrown and she began an ambitious project to restore them to their former glory. She is responsible for the climbing roses, the yew trees, herbaceous borders, delphiniums and clematis, making it one of the most romantic gardens in Britain.

MELBOURNE HALL
AND GARDENS

MELBOURNE, DERBYSHIRE

The gardens are off the B587, 8 miles to the south of Derby.

London and Wise designed Melbourne Hall, described as high Baroque or French in style. Sir Thomas Coke designed the gardens in 1704 and was also heavily influenced by French style. There is a birdcage arbour by the lake, a yew tunnel, and terraces leading to the lake, ponds, streams and magnificent herbaceous borders. The garden also has parterre and lead statuary. It was the former home of Lord Melbourne, who was Prime Minister when Queen Victoria came to the throne in 1837.

RENISHAW HALL
GARDENS

ECKINGTON, SHEFFIELD, DERBYSHIRE

The gardens are 6 miles to the southeast of Sheffield and 6 miles to the northeast of Chesterfield.

Sir George Sitwell laid out these gardens in a classical Italian style in 1895. The gardens have been well maintained and restored, showing their geometric design, yew hedges, statues and pyramids. There are wide, mixed borders, exotic plants and rose gardens. The camellias are especially appealing in the spring. The garden also has naturalistic planting with unusual shrubs, rambling roses and specimen trees. The original Renishaw design included terraces, pools and steps – ideas taken from Sitwell's visits to over 200 Italian gardens.

$\mathscr{S}$TAFFORDSHIRE

BIDDULPH GRANGE GARDEN

GRANGE ROAD, BIDDULPH, NEAR STOKE-ON-TRENT, STAFFORDSHIRE

The gardens are 8 miles to the north of Stoke-on-Trent.

These gardens are probably one of the most exciting and unusual English examples of the mixed style. There is an Italian garden, an American garden, a Chinese garden and an Egyptian garden. In essence, the gardens are a series of connected, compartmentalised areas, displaying a wide range of different specimens and planting styles. There are superb examples of bedding plants and herbaceous borders. High points are the Egyptian temple, the icehouse and the foundation. James and Maria Bateman created the gardens in the mid-19th century.

ALTON TOWERS GARDEN

ALTON, STAFFORDSHIRE

The gardens are signposted from junction 16 of the M6 and junction 28 of the M1 and are 18 miles to the east of Stoke-on-Trent.

Although Alton Towers is now a popular theme park, the garden was actually begun in the 15th century, by the highly eccentric Earl of Shrewsbury. It is said that the earl consulted known experts at the time, only to avoid their advice. It is a very early example of the mixed style and has an extremely diverse appearance. There is a monument copied from Athens, a pagoda and foundation, a Dutch garden, a replica Stonehenge and a Swiss cottage in the gardens.

SHUGBOROUGH GARDEN

GREAT HAYWOOD, MILFORD, STAFFORDSHIRE

The gardens are 6 miles to the east of Stafford, on the A513.

This 18th century garden has formal terraces with grey foliage, yellow roses and lavender. It also has a Victorian style rose garden. The rhododendrons dominate in spring and early summer. The garden also has a remarkable collection of early garden buildings, including a Chinese house and bridge, a temple, ruins and a Doric-style temple. Graham Stuart designed the rose garden in 1966 and the terraced garden was created in 1872. There are also wonderful herbaceous borders and an extensive woodland walk.

$\mathscr{S}$HROPSHIRE

HODNET HALL GARDENS

HODNET, MARKET DRAYTON, SHROPSHIRE

The gardens are 12 miles to the northeast of Shrewsbury, on the A53.

The Victorian house was designed by Anthony Salvin in 1870 and is set in 60 acres of woodland, with a superb display of rhododendrons, bluebells, camellia, azaleas and magnolias. The gardens are also famed for their extensive collection of specimen trees, as well as ornamental pools and flowering shrubs. Closer to the house are old-fashioned roses and mixed borders and in late summer there are stunning displays of hydrangeas. The site has a Tudor dovecote and lake within the woodland gardens.

WOLLERTON OLD HALL GARDEN

WOLLERTON, MARKET DRAYTON, SHROPSHIRE

The gardens are 14 miles to the northeast of Shrewsbury, off the A53.

Although John and Lesley Jenkins began the present garden in 1984, it is believed that there has been a garden here for over 500 years. The gardens surround a 16th century house, but the gardens themselves are very much in the Arts and Crafts tradition. The gardens extend to around three acres, consisting of a formal design with several different gardens, each with their own distinct character. The planting emphasises colour and form using many perennials along with unusual and rare species.

BIRMINGHAM and the WEST MIDLANDS

BIRMINGHAM BOTANICAL GARDENS

WESTBOURNE ROAD, EDGBASTON, BIRMINGHAM

The gardens can be found 2 miles to the southwest of the centre of Birmingham.

J. C. Loudon designed the Birmingham Botanical Gardens in 1829, and although he proposed the building of a circular house, there is now just a conservatory at the top of the site. The Botanical Gardens have the appearance of a Victorian public park, complete with a bandstand. In front of the conservatory is a lawn which slopes down, surrounded by shrubs and flowerbeds. There is a pinetum, a conifer grove with redwoods, cedars, pines, larches and firs, an alpine display, a herb garden and historic gardens representing Roman, medieval and Tudor planting.

ARWICKSHIRE

CHARLECOTE PARK
WELLESBOURNE, WARWICKSHIRE

The park is 6 miles to the south of Warwick, a mile west of Wellesbourne.

This huge house, in Elizabethan style, was begun in 1551 and boasts an especially fine gatehouse. During the 18th century it was essentially a deer park, with Capability Brown designing the grounds in 1756. He carried out most of the planting and widened the River Avon to give a more natural effect. During the 19th century a terraced garden was built between the house and the river. The park covers 188 acres and the National Trust has run it since 1946.

UPTON HOUSE GARDEN
BANBURY, WARWICKSHIRE BORDER

The garden can be found 7 miles to the northwest of Banbury, on the A422.

Upton House was built in 1695, but substantially altered in 1927 when a terrace was built in front of the house. The steps lead down to a lawn and a narrow valley, which extends across the gardens. The terraces tumble down towards a pool. One of the terraces contains a National Collection of asters. There is a large kitchen garden, still used to grow fruit and vegetables, along with huge herbaceous borders, a long Mediterranean border and a rose garden enclosed by yew.

BADDESLEY CLINTON HOUSE

RISING LANE, BADDESLEY, CLINTON VILLAGE, NOWLE, SOLIHULL, WARWICKSHIRE

The garden can be found 6 miles south of junction 5 of the M42.

These gardens surround an 18th century moated manor house and include a wildflower and meadow garden, ponds, woodland and lakeside walks and a formal courtyard garden. The walled garden dates from the early 18th century and shrub roses surround a sundial. The gardens are renowned for their dahlias, herbs and a Japanese bridge, which links the ponds to the nature trails. The house itself has changed little since 1634, when it was a haven for persecuted Catholics – there are three priest holes.

PACKWOOD HOUSE GARDEN

LAPWORTH, SOLIHULL, WARWICKSHIRE

The garden is 11 miles to the southeast of the centre of Birmingham.

The gardens at Packwood date from 1650 to 1660. They are particularly renowned for the yew garden, which is supposed to represent the Sermon on the Mount. There is a large, single yew on a tall mound, which is reached by a spiral path, with 12 large yews on the terrace below. There is another garden surrounded by a 17th century brick wall. There are also fine, herbaceous gardens, a Roman-style bath, a sunken pool and lakeside walks.

WORCESTERSHIRE

BURFORD HOUSE GARDENS

TENBURY WELLS, WORCESTERSHIRE

The gardens are just off the A40, between Oxford and Cheltenham.

The gardens at Burford have seven acres of lawn and borders alongside the banks of the River Teme. An early Georgian house is surrounded by gardens designed by John Treasure in 1952. The gardens hold the National Collection of clematis, of which 500 varieties are on show. There are 2,000 other varieties of plants, including huge wisteria, which have thrived there since 1960. Beyond a Georgian, turfed bridge an area of wildflowers and meadow is a stunning contrast to the regimented nature of the remaining gardens.

SPETCHLEY PARK GARDENS

SPETCHLEY, WORCESTERSHIRE

The gardens can be found 2 miles to the east of Worcester, on the A422.

This Georgian house was originally a deer park with a lake, but boasts a Victorian-style garden. Rose Berkeley and her sister, Ellen Wilmott, the renowned Edwardian gardener, designed the gardens. The gardens were developed by the family over a number of years and now contain many rare and unusual trees, shrubs and plants. There is a huge collection of daffodils, which are best seen in April, and wonderful walks through the deer park, garden lake and walled gardens.

# HEREFORDSHIRE

BRYANS GROUND

LETCHMORE LANE, STAPLETON, NEAR PRESTEIGNE, HEREFORDSHIRE

The gardens are off the B4362, just outside Presteigne.

Bryans Ground is, in essence, the idyllic Edwardian garden. Although the house dates to 1911, the gardens were only developed since 1993. There are three acres of intimate garden 'rooms' in the Arts and Crafts tradition. The owners, David Wheeler and Simon Dorrell, have created all of this. It is a garden to savour, with stunning architectural features incorporating follies, towers, topiary, pools, a potager and fragrant flowers. There are now five acres of specimen trees along the riverbank.

HERGEST CROFT GARDENS

KINGTON, HEREFORDSHIRE

The gardens are half a mile west of Kington, off the A44.

The Edwardian house is surrounded by 50 acres of gardens in four distinct sections, boasting some 4,000 rare shrubs and trees. The kitchen garden has an avenue of ancient apple trees and 36 metre (120 foot) herbaceous borders, a rose garden as well as a fruit and vegetable garden. Cedars and the National Collection of birches dominate the Azalea Garden, whilst the Park Wood is full of ancient oaks, exotic trees and rhododendrons. Magnolias, cherries and hydrangeas surround the house itself.

GLOUCESTERSHIRE

HIDCOTE MANOR GARDENS

CHIPPING CAMPDEN, GLOUCESTERSHIRE

The gardens are 4 miles to the northeast of Chipping Campden, a mile to the east of the B4632.

The gardens at Hidcote were created around 1905 by the plantsman Major Lawrence Johnston. The gardens are best described as being in the Arts and Crafts tradition, with yew and beech hedges creating a series of garden 'rooms'. The gardens are particularly famous for their rare shrubs and trees, but the herbaceous borders and collection of old roses are equally as stunning. A circular, raised pond occupies one of the many 'rooms'. Overall, the gardens have superb craftsmanship.

SNOWSHILL MANOR GARDEN

SNOWSHILL, GLOUCESTERSHIRE

The garden is 3 miles southwest of Broadway, off the A44.

Snowshill Manor is a Tudor house with an 18th century façade and a garden in the Arts and Crafts tradition. William Morris and medieval craftsmanship heavily influenced the designers, Charles Wade and Baillie Scott. The garden consists of a number of discrete garden enclosures and highly imaginative planting. The gardens extend to two acres and are now organic, showing stunning borders, water features and magnificent vistas. In many respects, Snowshill rivals nearby Hidcote, both in design and beauty.

PAINSWICK ROCOCO GARDEN

THE STABLES, PAINSWICK HOUSE, PAINSWICK, GLOUCESTERSHIRE

The gardens can be found half a mile to the northwest of Painswick, on the B4073.

The rococo gardens at Painswick are unique and fully restored using a painting by Thomas Robins dating to 1748. The gardens encompass the Red House folly, a superb kitchen garden, three further follies (the Gothic Alcove, Eagle House and Exedta) and a maze built to celebrate the garden's 250th anniversary. The gardens, in six acres, are in a secluded Cotswold valley. Restoration work began in the 1970s, when the garden was overgrown and abandoned, but now visitors can see the true historical value.

WESTBURY COURT GARDEN

WESTBURY-ON-SEVERN, GLOUCESTERSHIRE

The gardens are 9 miles to the southwest of Gloucester, on the A48.

This formal Dutch garden, or court water garden, was laid out between 1696 and 1705. It contains many plants brought to England before 1700. Westbury has a pavilion and two canals, with the pavilion at the head of one and the other bordered by yew hedging. The garden was restored after it came into possession of the National Trust in 1967. The garden has, arguably, the oldest holm oak in the country and a stunning secret walled garden, which should not be missed.

BARNSLEY HOUSE GARDEN

THE CLOSE, BARNSLEY, GLOUCESTERSHIRE

The garden is in Barnsley village, 4 miles northeast of Cirencester, on the B4425.

Barnsley House and gardens is a fascinating fusion of a William and Mary building and an Arts and Crafts garden. The garden is partly walled and was designed in 1951 by Rosemary Verey, in the Gertrude Jekyll style. It boasts a lime walk, ornamental vegetable garden, lily pond and statuary. The house, made from Cotswold stone, is surrounded by four acres, best described as gardens within gardens, with colourful borders and, of course, a knot garden, which should not be overlooked.

KIFTSGATE COURT GARDENS

CHIPPING CAMPDEN, GLOUCESTERSHIRE

The gardens are 4 miles northeast of Chipping Campden, near Hidcote Garden.

These gardens were completed between the end of the 19th century and the beginning of the 20th century. Heather Muir designed them, with assistance from Major Johnston from Hidcote. As such, they are Arts and Crafts in appearance, with herbaceous borders, a four square garden, a rockery, a yellow border, a white garden, lawns and a bluebell wood. Overall, there are harmonious colour schemes, but the roses are the show-stealers. Bulbs and tender plants nestle in the lower and sunken gardens.

$\mathcal{O}$XFORDSHIRE

PUSEY HOUSE GARDEN
PUSEY, OXFORDSHIRE

The garden is 15 miles from junction 15 of the M4.

Pusey is a tiny village of some 20 Georgian houses. The big house itself has a long and varied history and has been owned by the Pusey family since the days of Cnut and was also the former home of Edward Pusey, the leader of the Oxford Movement. The grounds around the house were created as a pleasure ground and landscape park. Some of the gardens date back to the 18th century, whilst other parts to around 1935 when Geoffrey Jellicoe made designs.

BLENHEIM PALACE GARDEN
WOODSTOCK, OXFORDSHIRE

The gardens are 8 miles to the northwest of Oxford, on the A44.

The palace, designed by Vanburgh around 1705, became the home of the Dukes of Marlborough. The stunning gardens developed during the 18th century and were ultimately transformed by Capability Brown. The formal gardens date to the 1920s, the water terraces to the 1930s and the arboretum saw Winston Churchill propose to Clementine Hozier. The rose garden gives way to the Grand Cascade, and in 2004 the secret garden opened after 30 years of neglect. Between 1893 and 1919 alone 455,000 trees were planted at Blenheim.

GREYS COURT GARDEN

ROTHERFIELD GREYS,
HENLEY-ON-THAMES, OXFORDSHIRE

The gardens are east of the B481, 3 miles to the west of Henley-on-Thames.

Greys Court is a picturesque 14th century house with a beautiful courtyard and a tower dated to 1347. The outbuildings include a Tudor wheelhouse, an icehouse and a maze. The house has a walled vegetable garden, with soft fruit and flower borders. There are a series of gardens set inside the medieval walls of the original courtyard, including a garden with box hedges, topiary and a Chinese-style bridge. Masses of colour come from bluebells, roses and snowdrops.

ROUSHAM HOUSE AND GARDEN

STEEPLE ASHTON, BICESTER, OXFORDSHIRE

The park is 12 miles to the north of Oxford, off the A4260.

This Jacobean-style manor house was built during the 1630s. In 1719, Colonel Robert Dormer inherited the house and engaged the royal gardener, Charles Bridgeman, to design the gardens. It was almost complete in 1737, and the following year William Kent was brought in to continue the work. Kent blended the garden into the landscape and transformed the nearby river. He had a mock medieval bridge built and a folly, known as 'Eyecatcher'. Rousham has the only untouched landscape garden to remain in England.

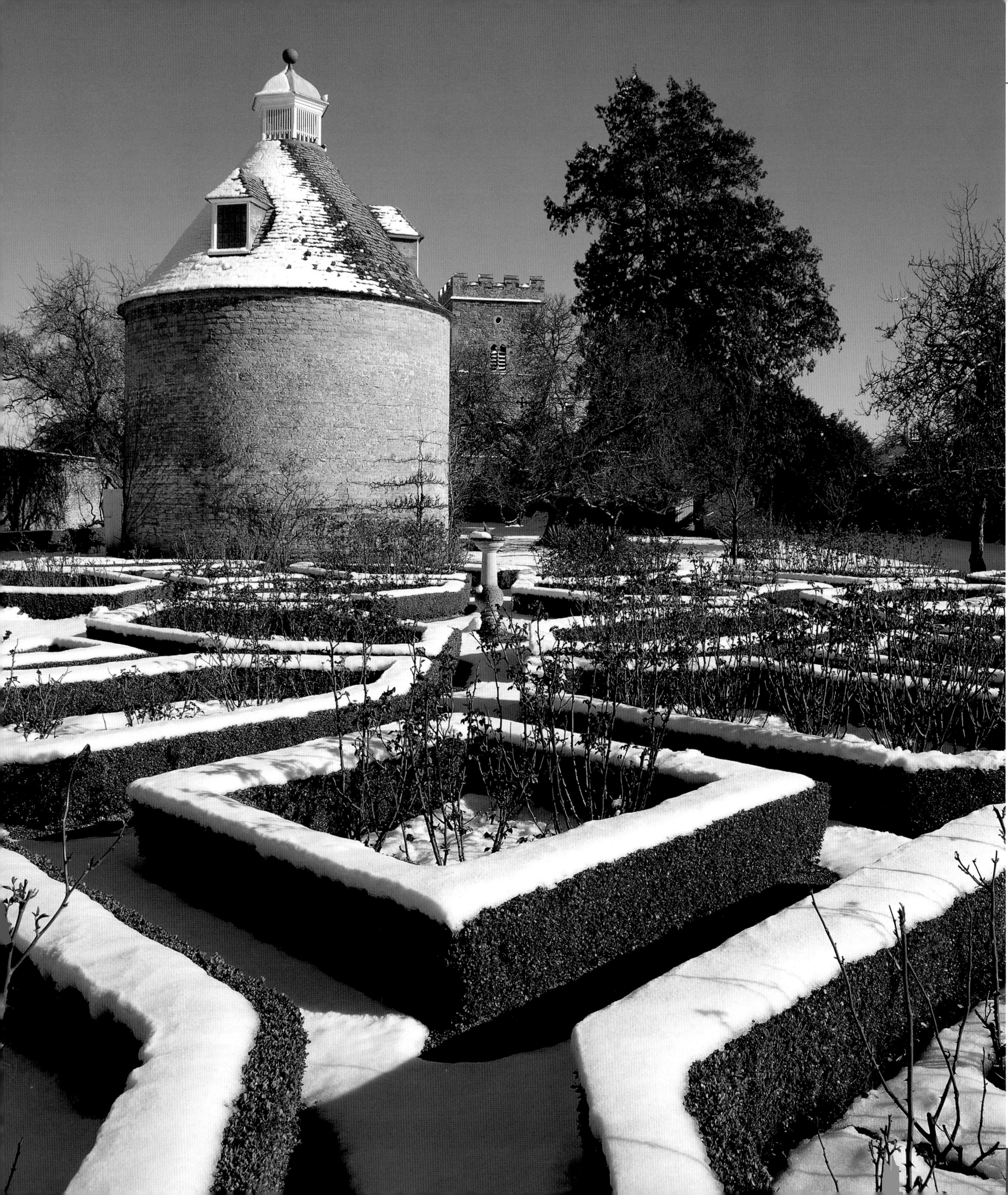

SOUTHEAST
of
ENGLAND

The southeast of England is the most densely populated area of Britain. It has a horseshoe-shaped ring of chalk downs and dramatic coastline cliffs. It is a vast swathe of counties, from Kent in the east to Berkshire and Buckinghamshire in the west.

This region is rich in gardens of all types. Varied gardens surround stately homes, castles and palaces. There are landscaped gardens, formal gardens and woodland gardens.

From the royal connections at Hampton Court, Richmond Park and Kew, there are wilder influences, such as West Wycombe Park, which was created by Sir Francis Dashwood, the founder of the Hellfire Club. All of the greatest garden designers have been at work in the southeast, including William Kent, James Gibbs, Geoffrey Jellicoe, Charles Bridgeman and Capability Brown.

The gardens range from the 1,000 acre parkland around Luton Hoo to far less expansive but equally as impressive, smaller sites, such as Saling Hall Garden. There is a garden created for the Queen Mother, another dedicated to the herbalist Nicholas Culpepper, one showing the genius of Vita Sackville-West and another the surrealist influence of Henry James. There are old gardens, new gardens and special collections, all captivating no matter what season.

Buckinghamshire

WEST WYCOMBE PARK

WEST WYCOMBE, BUCKINGHAMSHIRE

The park is 2 miles to the west of High Wycombe.

Sir Francis Dashwood, the founder of the Hellfire Club, created the house and gardens here in the 18th century. There is a landscaped garden now on the site of an earlier geometrical garden. Thomas Cook designed the landscaped garden very much in the style of Capability Brown, incorporating small temples and garden buildings. Humphry Repton was also involved in some of the design work. The property, owned by the National Trust, retains its perfectly preserved rococo landscape, set within the Chiltern's countryside.

CLIVEDEN GARDEN

TAPLOW, MAIDENHEAD, BUCKINGHAMSHIRE

The gardens are 2 miles to the north of Taplow, off junction 7 of the M4 or junction 4 of the M40.

The original house, built on a high, wooded plateau overlooking the Thames, was constructed in 1666. Charles Bridgeman created the walks and avenues, but Sir Charles Barry designed the present house in 1849 and construction began two years later. It was once the home of Lady Astor. The garden is of a mixed style, dating to the 19th century, with Sir Geoffrey Jellicoe designing the rose garden in 1959. The gardens have topiary, statuary, a parterre, water gardens and woodland and riverside walks.

STOWE LANDSCAPE GARDENS

BUCKINGHAM, BUCKINGHAMSHIRE

The gardens are 3 miles to the northwest of Buckingham.

Originally Stowe had an English Baroque garden, typified in the 1690s by a parterre garden. Between 1710–20, Charles Bridgeman as the garden architect and John Vanburgh as the general architect designed a new park. William Kent and James Gibbs took over in the 1730s, adding temples. Then Capability Brown took over, creating a Grecian valley and giving Bridgeman's original octagonal pond and 11-acre lake a more natural shape. Most of the buildings and garden have been restored and thousands of shrubs and trees planted.

HUGHENDEN PARK
HIGH WYCOMBE, BUCKINGHAMSHIRE

The garden is off the A4128, 1.5 miles to the north of High Wycombe.

The manor has a high Victorian, mixed-style garden, which was originally designed for the then Prime Minister Benjamin Disraeli, whose wife, Mary Anne, designed the terrace and had a very hands-on approach to the restoration. There is formal bedding dating to the 1880s, which is now being restored by the National Trust. The orchard, which has also been restored, contains 35 varieties of apple and four varieties of pear. There are woodland walks and many unusual plants within the gardens.

CHENIES MANOR HOUSE
RICKMANSWORTH, BUCKINGHAMSHIRE

The gardens are on the A404, 4 miles to the east of Amersham.

This is an early Tudor, brick built house with a fortified tower and was formerly the home of the Russells, later the Dukes of Bedford. It was much visited by both Henry VIII and Elizabeth I. More recently, the later Arts and Crafts garden, with a sunken garden, topiary, fountain court, physic garden and herbaceous borders, has appeared on many television programmes. It has two mazes, one of which was created in 1991, and a magnificent tulip display.

EDFORDSHIRE

THE SWISS GARDEN

BIGGLESWADE ROAD, OLD WARDEN, BIGGLESWADE, BEDFORDSHIRE

This garden is 1.5 miles to the west of Biggleswade.

This 10 acre, mixed style Swiss garden was designed around 1800 and incorporates thatched cottages, ponds, bridges and a grotto. It was created by Lord Ongley and combines his fleeting passion for picturesque architecture and ornamental gardening. There are tiny islands and ponds, intricate ironwork bridges and magnificent shrubs and rare trees. The Swiss Cottage itself, with its wonderful fretwork, perches on a grassy knoll at the centre of this romantic garden. John Buonarotti Papworth, who lived close by, probably designed it.

LUTON HOO

LUTON, BEDFORDSHIRE

The garden lies to the southeast of Luton, off the A1081.

Robert Adam designed this palatial mansion for the 3rd Earl of Bute in 1767. It was rebuilt after a fire in 1843 and remodelled once again in 1903. It has wonderful views over 1,000 acres of parkland, designed by Capability Brown. The garden flourished until the late 19th century and is now overgrown and in the process of being restored. There are examples of Victorian and Edwardian glasshouses and a six acre hexagonal wall garden. The mansion now belongs to a hotel group.

ERTFORDSHIRE

HATFIELD HOUSE GARDENS

HATFIELD, HERTFORDSHIRE

The gardens can be found 1 mile to east of junction 4 of the A1M.

No less than three major designers were involved in the creation of this Jacobean garden, which surrounds an Elizabethan house. Thomas Chaundler, Salomon de Caus and John Tradescant created the 17th century character of the site. The garden has terraces, enclosures, a privy garden, herb garden and knot garden. Extending to around 42 acres, the park is heavily wooded with an avenue of ancient oaks. The formal parterres lead down to the lake and the wilderness areas will always provide tranquillity and surprises.

KNEBWORTH HOUSE PARK AND GARDENS

NEAR STEVENAGE, HERTFORDSHIRE

The gardens are 2 miles to the south of Stevenage.

Although the house is Victorian, the gardens at Knebworth date back to the 1600s. It was once the home of Edward Bulwer-Lytton and Lord Lytton. When Edwin Lutyens married into the family he modified the garden. The pergola, the lawn surrounded by rose beds, the pollarded limes and the gold garden were all his design. Gertrude Jekyll designed the herb garden in 1907 but it was not constructed until 1982. Massive restoration has been underway since 1980, restoring the original features.

ST PAUL'S WALDEN BURY GARDEN

WHITWELL, NEAR HITCHIN, HERTFORDSHIRE

The garden is on the B561, 5 miles to the south of Hitchin.

This 19th century Grade I house is surrounded by gardens representing the forest style popular in the 1730s. Geoffrey Jellicoe designed one of the glades. The house was the birthplace and childhood home of Queen Elizabeth the Queen Mother. One childhood connection is the statue group of a woman and child, named 'Charity', which she had copied and placed in the garden of the Royal Lodge in Windsor Great Park. The enclosed garden has avenues, viewpoints and is lined with beech hedges.

SSEX

HYDE HALL GARDEN
RETTENDON, NEAR CHELMSFORD, ESSEX

The garden is 2 miles to the east of Rettendon.

Dr and Mrs Robinson acquired this Essex farmhouse in 1955 and from an unpromising start. From only six trees and no garden, they created lawns, a dell, raised beds, mixed borders and a lily pond. The Royal Horticultural Society now runs the garden. It has a wonderful spring garden, a lake and the National Collection of viburnum. It is a dynamic garden, constantly changing to meet the challenges of the site and soil, proving that hard work can triumph over the most difficult conditions.

SALING HALL GARDEN
GREAT SALING, NEAR BRAINTREE, ESSEX

The gardens are 6 miles to the northwest of Braintree, 2 miles north of the A120

Hugh Johnson has extensively redesigned this 17th century manor house since 1971. It is essentially a 12 acre arboretum, with an extensive collection of pines, sorbus, robinias, prunus and a host of other varieties. There are cedars from Oregon, a weeping juniper and many unusual pines. The fruit trees have been shaped into mushrooms and there are clipped cypress and a line of Irish junipers. The borders are distinctly Mediterranean and there is a vegetable garden, water garden, valley garden and a Japanese garden.

GIBBERD GARDEN

MARSH LANE, GILDEN WAY, HARLOW, ESSEX

*The garden can be reached by taking junction 7 of the M11
and then the A414 to Harlow, into the B183.*

In 1946 Sir Frederick Gibberd was appointed the master planner of the new town of Harlow. He designed this garden on the outskirts of Harlow in the 1950s and continued work there until his death in 1984. The gardens are a series of rooms with pools, alleys, groves and glades. Scattered amongst the gardens are 50 sculptures, architectural salvage, a moated castle, a gazebo and large ceramic pots. The garden is situated on the side of a small valley, which slopes down to Pincey Brook.

LONDON

ISABELLA PLANTATION
RICHMOND PARK, RICHMOND, LONDON

The plantation covers the southern third of Richmond Park.

Richmond Park itself covers 2,360 acres and was originally a hunting park for Charles I. In 1637 he established herds of fallow and red deer, which still roam the park. The plantation is essentially a woodland garden and arguably has the best selection of rhododendrons and azaleas within the London area. They are at their best in late spring and early summer. Overall, the plantation has 40 acres of lawns, streams, ponds and glades, including a bog garden with primula and flowering heathers.

THE ROYAL BOTANICAL GARDENS
KEW, RICHMOND, LONDON

The gardens can be accessed from Kew Green, near Kew Bridge.

Kew Gardens is a World Heritage Site and the site of a royal residence, now charting 250 years of historical gardens. It has a virtually unrivalled collection of 30,000 types of plant from all around the world. The original gardens were created for Augusta, Princess of Wales, to surround Kew Palace, her home. Sir William Chambers carried out much of the original design in a very oriental style. It was he who designed the Chinese pagoda and several of the other buildings.

MIDDLESEX

HAMPTON COURT PALACE GARDEN

EAST MOSELY, MIDDLESEX

The garden can be found at the junction of the A308 and the A309, on the north side of the Kingston Bridge.

The Hampton Court gardens are essentially Renaissance in style, as Henry VIII had them built in the 1530s. They were converted between 1660 and 1702, first by Charles II, who employed John Rose to construct a canal, and later by William of Orange. William employed George London and Daniel Marot to create a network of avenues and parterres. The gardens extend to 60 acres and there is a famous maze. The world's oldest vine can still be seen here, which produces 315 kg (700 lbs) of grapes every year.

SYON PARK GARDENS

BRENTFORD, MIDDLESEX

The garden is 2 miles to the west of Kew Bridge.

During the mid-18th century, Capability Brown landscaped the Syon Park and sited the collection of rare trees. The park extends to 40 acres, but now the dominant style is that of the 19th century. The garden has a domed and galleried conservatory, shown here, which was created by Charles Fowler in the 1820s. There is also a lake, a circular pool, a Doric column, a rose garden and water meadows with stunning views towards the River Thames. The house is of Tudor origins with later additions.

BERKSHIRE

SAVILL GARDEN AND VALLEY GARDEN

WINDSOR GREAT PARK, WINDSOR, BERKSHIRE

The gardens are 5 miles from Windsor.

Savill Garden extends to some 35 acres and is, in effect, a large woodland garden, rather like a public park, with a wide range of trees, shrubs, herbaceous plants and a central lake. The magnolias, camellias, azaleas and rhododendrons dominate in spring. In the summer the herbaceous gardens, roses and alpines take centre stage. Extensive gold and russet foliage abounds in the autumn and in the winter the bare trees, with their delicate branches and stunning bark, dominate the scene.

HAMPSHIRE/ ISLE OF WIGHT

OSBORNE HOUSE

EAST COWES, ISLE OF WIGHT

The gardens are 1 mile to the southeast of East Cowes.

After her marriage to Prince Albert in 1840, Queen Victoria engaged Thomas Cubitt, a well known London builder, to create her family residence in the country. In essence, the gardens are in the Victorian/Italian style. Prince Albert and Cubitt designed the terraces. The house and grounds extend to 1,000 acres, including several acres of trees, which include a Swiss chalet that was imported as a playhouse for their children. Queen Victoria died there in 1901, a place she always considered home.

MOTTISTONE MANOR GARDENS

MOTTISTONE, ISLE OF WIGHT

The gardens are 2 miles west of Brighstone.

In 1086 the manor belonged to William the Conqueror and in 1212 it became a priory, dissolved by Thomas Cromwell in 1536. The house was remodelled in the 1740s. Since the early 19th century, when Gilbert Russell, a descendent of the founder of the priory, acquired the house, it has acquired open lawns enclosed by stands of trees. The National Trust acquired the house and gardens in 1957 and, under the direction of Graham Stuart Thomas, paths, hedging, roses and other new features were added.

THE HILLIER GARDEN

JERMYNS LANE, AMPFIELD, ROMSEY, HAMPSHIRE

*The gardens are situated between the villages of Ampfield and Braishfield,
3 miles to the northeast of Romsey.*

In 1953 the Hillier family began transforming the land around their home. In 1977, after 25 years of work, the house and gardens were given to Hampshire County Council. The collection includes 42,000 plants from 12,000 different types in a 180 acre site. One of the latest additions is the Winter Garden, which was opened in 1988 and contains 650 different types of winter plants. The Gurkha Memorial Garden, on three levels, contains unique flora from Nepal and was opened in 1997.

HOUGHTON LODGE GARDEN

STOCKBRIDGE, HAMPSHIRE

The garden is 1.5 miles to the south of Stockbridge, off the A30.

Extensive grounds surround this 18th century Gothic cottage with lawns sweeping down to the River Test. The gardens contain many original trees and shrubs; there are wonderful herbaceous borders and topiary examples. The walled garden and hydroponic greenhouse have been fully restored and there is a woodland walk, river walks and an orchid house. In addition to the informal gardens there is a walled kitchen garden containing peach and pear trees, a herb garden, roses, buddleia, peony and soft fruits.

EXBURY GARDENS

EXBURY, HAMPSHIRE

The gardens are 15 miles to the southwest of Southampton.

This 200 acre woodland garden is most well known for the Rothschild collection of rhododendrons, azaleas and camellias. This is not the only attraction, as there is also a wonderful daffodil meadow, deep herbaceous borders, exotic trees, rare shrubs, a rock garden and a rose garden. There are several ponds, one of which is spanned by a Japanese bridge. The Lovers' Lane leads towards the Beaulieu River, flanked by azaleas. The house itself was built in the 1920s and is faced with Portland stone.

HINTON AMPNER

BRAMDEAN, NEAR ALRESFORD, HAMPSHIRE

The gardens are 8 miles east of Winchester.

The 18th century house and 20th century garden were designed by Ralph Dutton and are now owned by the National Trust. Dutton was interested in shrubs and this shows in the overall design of the gardens. There are walks and terraces with intricate planting, topiary, hedges and ornaments. The garden is extremely tranquil and has unexpected views of the wonderful countryside, highly scented plants and shrubs with fascinating pastel shades. Above all it is a shrub garden, with interest all year round.

MOTTISFONT ABBEY
MOTTISFONT, NEAR ROMSEY, HAMPSHIRE

The garden is 4.5 miles northwest of Romsey.

This former Augustinian priory overlooks the River Test and has numerous ancient trees and an 18th century summer house. The rose garden was designed and planted by Graham Stuart Thomas. Geoffrey Jellicoe created the lime walk in 1936. It is the rose garden that steals the show, with old-fashioned pre-1900 varieties, possessing incredible scents and trailing from the walls, arches and pergolas. The lavender walk is a wonderful bonus, and in addition there are colourful herbaceous borders and a lavender parterre.

SURREY

HATCHLANDS PARK
EAST CLANDON, SURREY

The park is 3 miles to the east of Guildford, on the A247.

The house was originally built in the 1750s and is set in a 430 acre site. At one time the building and grounds belonged to Goodhart-Rendl, who was an architectural historian. There is a garden designed by Gertrude Jekyll, which has been planted using her original 1914 plans. There is also an area of the garden that has been restored to Humphry Repton's original designs. The garden overlooks woods and has stone ornaments, a temple, a fountain and a terrace.

LOSELEY PARK
NEAR GUILDFORD, SURREY

The park is off the B3000, 3 miles to the southeast of Guildford.

This Elizabethan house was built around 1562 and has a lawn that gives way to a moat, a walled garden, yew hedges and herbaceous plants. There are a series of rooms that include a rose garden with over 1,000 plants. The flower garden has a maze of pathways, and there is a white garden with fountains and a herb garden. The 2.5 acre walled garden is based on a design by Gertrude Jekyll. There is a vine walk, ancient wisteria and mulberry trees.

CLAREMONT LANDSCAPE GARDEN

PORTSMOUTH ROAD, ESHER, SURREY

The gardens are on the east of the A306, to the south of Esher.

The gardens at Claremont are considered to be some of the finest and possibly the first of the English landscape style. The park was originally part of a much larger estate. Charles Bridgeman originally laid it out for John Vanbrugh, and it contain a grass amphitheatre and a belvedere. Around 1735, William Kent began to transform the garden. He had converted the canal into a lake, adding an island with a pavilion. He serpentined the lake and restored the amphitheatre.

POLESDEN LACY

GREAT BOOKHAM, NEAR DORKING, SURREY

The garden is 5 miles to the northwest of Dorking.

The house was originally a Regency villa, constructed between 1821 and 1823. The Edwardian hostess, Mrs Ronald Grevill, extensively remodelled it between 1906 and 1909 in order to house her furniture, paintings, porcelain and silver. The grounds are vast, extending to 1,400 acres and the National Trust now owns them. The gardens are in the Arts and Craft style, designed by J. Cheal & Sons. There are a series of walled and hedged enclosures, with roses and herbaceous plants.

WINKWORTH ARBORETUM

HASCOMBE ROAD, GODALMING, SURREY

The gardens are on the east side of the B2130, 2 miles to the southeast of Godalming.

Gertrude Jekyll lived here as a child and saw the woodland garden before it was planted with exotic species during the late 1930s by Dr Wilfred Fox. Over the years, the many rare specimens have developed into a fascinating woodland landscape and although the soil is sandy and dry, the plants and trees thrive. There are two lakes, cedars, maples, azaleas, bluebells and rhododendrons. There are over 1,000 different shrubs and trees, stunning spring flowers and amazing autumn colours.

WISLEY RHS GARDEN

WISLEY, NEAR WOKING, SURREY

The gardens are on the northwest of the A3, 7 miles to the north of Guildford.

Wisley Garden was originally established by George Wilson, an avid horticulturalist, and given to the Royal Horticultural Society in 1903. In 1911 Edward White designed the rock garden. Later, heather, bog and woodland gardens were created. In the 1960s Lanning Roper created the walled canal garden. The development of the site continues and in addition to the huge plant collection there are many demonstration gardens. The greenhouses have orchids, cacti and tropical plants and there are wonderful water features and woodland walks.

ENT

DODDINGTON PLACE

DODDINGTON, NEAR SITTINGBOURNE, KENT

The gardens are 6 miles to the south of Sittingbourne.

The building was created in 1870 and the Croft family, sherry importers, owned it between 1870 and 1905. The gardens extend to 10 acres and were created by William Nesfield. The folly was built in 1997 as a memorial to Alexandra Oldfield, who belonged to the family of joint owners of the house. The folly is octagonal, two-storey and brick-built. The woodland garden is spectacular in spring; there are mixed borders in the formal terraces, an Edwardian rock garden, lawns and yew hedges.

PENSHURST PLACE GARDEN

PENSHURST, TONBRIDGE, KENT

The gardens are 4 miles to the southeast of Tonbridge, on the B2167.

The Tudor gardens at Penshurst surround a 14th century manor house. The gardens were restored for the first time in the 1860s, using an engraving dated to around 1700. A second restoration project was begun in the 1970s. The gardens consist of a series of rectangular enclosures, including a rose garden, an orchard and a box parterre. Lanning Roper designed the rose garden. There are innumerable flowering bulbs in spring and orchard fruits, roses and herbaceous borders in the summer months.

WALMER CASTLE

WALMER, DEAL, KENT

The gardens are 2 miles to the south of Deal.

Originally a Tudor fort, Walmer Castle was later converted into a stately home. It was once the royal residence of the Lords Warden of the Cinque Ports. It has an Arts and Crafts garden, which was created for the Queen Mother by Penelope Hobhouse to celebrate her 95th birthday. There is a canal with a herbaceous border, a long broad walk also with extensive herbaceous borders, a kitchen garden, drifts of daffodils, a wildflower meadow, a moat garden and a woodland walk.

SISSINGHURST CASTLE
SISSINGHURST, CRANBROOK, KENT

The castle garden is a mile to the east of Sissinghurst village.

In 1930, Harold Nicolson and Vita Sackville-West bought the sadly dilapidated castle and grounds of Sissinghurst. Early on they designed the garden and the plan was strictly adhered to over the following years. The garden represents a truly English style, particularly in the renowned White Garden, shown above. It has a profusion of old roses climbing over walls and even dominating the trees. The nuttery boasts primroses and polyanthus and the lime walk, spring bulbs. The roses dominate throughout June and July, with thousands blooming everywhere.

LEEDS CASTLE GARDENS
MAIDSTONE, KENT

The gardens are 6 miles to the east of Maidstone.

This former royal palace would once have had medieval or Tudor gardens, but within the five acres of wooded grounds there is a wide variety of different styles. There is a Nicholas Culpepper herbal garden and a maze and grotto that date to the 1980s. The Lady Baillie Garden is in a red brick Arts and Crafts style and overlooks the lake. The gardens have the National Collections of nepetas and monardos. There are wonderful rose gardens and beautiful herbaceous borders.

USSEX

WEST DEAN GARDENS

WEST DEAN, CHICHESTER, SUSSEX

The gardens are 6 miles north of Chichester, on the A286.

James Wyatt designed the 19th century Gothic house of West Dean and Harold Peto created the 20th century Arts and Craft garden in 1911. Henry James, an admirer of surrealist art, lived here, and one of his lasting features is a huge stone pergola with timber beams. In recent years the kitchen garden and the glasshouses have been fully restored, and they have a wide variety of different plants. There is a sunken garden with a pond, a park and woodland garden, set in a valley location.

SHEFFIELD PARK GARDEN

NEAR UCKFIELD, SUSSEX

The garden is 5 miles to the northwest of Uckfield, east of the A275.

Capability Brown created this magnificent landscaped garden around 1775. Since then, a 20th century woodland garden and arboretum have been added. The 3rd Earl of Sheffield and Arthur Soames owned the estate between the latter part of the 19th century and the mid-20th century. The former created the bridge, cascade and Middle Lake and the latter the shrubs, particularly the rhododendrons. There are huge displays of daffodils and bluebells in spring, with azaleas and rhododendrons in the summer.

NYMANS GARDEN

HANDCROSS, NEAR HAYWARDS HEATH, SUSSEX

The garden is just off the M23, 4.5 miles to the south of Crawley.

Ludwig Messel began Nymans Garden in 1890, focusing on magnolias, heathers and camellias. He used the skills of William Robinson for the herbaceous borders and topiary. The manor house is 14th century, but it was gutted by fire in 1947. The Messel family sent plant hunters around the world to bring together their collection of magnolias and rhododendrons. The result is that there are not only magnificent borders in the summer, but also a huge variety of colour all year round, including the winter.

LEONARDS LEE

LOWER BREEDING, HORSHAM, SUSSEX

The gardens are 3 miles to the southwest of Handcross.

This 240 acre valley site has no less than seven lakes. Richard Payne Knight, Sir Uvedale Price and J. C. Loudon inspired it and Sir Edmund Loder purchased the estate in 1889. There are enormous numbers of camellias, rhododendrons and magnolias. In spring there are azaleas and bluebells, and throughout the summer there are flowering trees and wildflowers. The gardens also have a rock garden, a bonsai collection and a herd of wallabies, which were imported by Loder shortly after he bought the house.

SOUTHWEST of ENGLAND

The southwest, extending from Cornwall into Wiltshire and to the borders of Wales, contains two of the most dramatic National Parks in the country, Dartmoor and Exmoor. There are 14 other areas of outstanding natural beauty and over 600 km (370 miles) of stunning coastline.

The landscape in this corner of the country is incredibly varied. There are the chalk lands of Wiltshire and Dorset, the valleys of Cornwall and Devon and the moorland in the National Parks, whilst Somerset and Avon are peat lands.

You will find 700 different types of rhododendron around an 18th century house near Bodmin, a jungle with pineapples near St Austell and futuristic biomes at the Eden Project. Near Torrington there is a garden with plants from Australia and New Zealand and at Chard, a monastery with famed topiary.

The ideas of the great designers are readily visible, including Gertrude Jekyll, Edwin Lutyens, Capability Brown, Harold Peto and Henry Repton. There are gardens inspired by monks, bankers influenced by Italian arts, lovers of follies and those with a passion for exotic, tender and rare plants and trees. Sufficient to match every need, and enough for a lifetime, the selection here is just a taste of the hundreds of gardens in the area.

CORNWALL

PENCARROW HOUSE GARDENS

BODMIN, CORNWALL

The garden is 4 miles from the northwest of Bodmin.

The gardens extend to some 50 acres and there are wonderful lawns, specimen trees, woodland walks and innumerable plants and shrubs. Spring sees the mile-long carriage drive framed with azaleas, rhododendrons, camellias, daffodils and primroses. The house dates to around 1760 and most of the garden to 1831. It has terraces, a fountain, icehouse, Italian garden, lake and rock garden. There are no less than 700 different types of rhododendrons, and blue hydrangeas dominate the views around the lake.

LANHYDROCK GARDEN

BODMIN, CORNWALL

The gardens are in Launceston.

The 30 acre gardens at Lanhydrock were begun in 1857, although there are many trees that date to as early as 1634. The old house was rebuilt in 1881, hence the gardens have a Victorian style. There are many magnolias, rhododendrons, herbaceous borders, formal gardens and camellias to be seen throughout the summer. Within the woodland walks there are many rare trees and flowering shrubs. The gardens also have Irish yews, a courtyard garden with roses, boxed edge beds and topiary.

GLENDURGAN GARDEN

MAWNAN SMITH, FALMOUTH, CORNWALL

The gardens are 4 miles to the southwest of Falmouth.

Between 1826 and 1833, Albert Fox began to develop this 30 acre woodland valley. It has especially good views of the Helford Estuary and being in a valley it has a relatively mild climate. This has allowed the planting of many exotic and rare trees, as well as shrubs. Above all, the garden is renowned for its rhododendrons, camellias, magnolias, wildflowers, azaleas, aquilegias, foxgloves and hydrangeas. There is a wonderful and challenging laurel maze, shown here, which is believed to have been planted by Alfred Fox in 1833.

THE EDEN PROJECT

BODELVA, ST AUSTELL, CORNWALL

The Eden Project is 4 miles to the east of St Austell, signposted from the A30, A390 and A391.

Built within a disused china clay pit, this 35 acre custom-made site opened in 2001. It was designed by Tom Smith and has the largest greenhouses in the world. The huge biomes are made from advanced construction materials. Rainforests are recreated in the humid tropics biome and plants from the Mediterranean, South Africa and California are in the warm temperature biome. A third outdoor zone contains plants happy with the Cornish weather and temperature. A new semi-arid biome is underway.

THE LOST GARDENS OF HELIGAN

PENTEWAN, ST AUSTELL, CORNWALL

The gardens are signposted from St Austell, on the B3273

These gardens were originally designed in 1790, but were left unkempt since 1914. Tim Smit and John Nelson rediscovered the garden in 1991. The garden is in two parts; the Northern Garden and the Jungle, the latter containing lakes and trees. The pineapples yielded 100 fruits in 1998, typical of the trees and shrubs brought to Heligan from all over the world. A full working Victorian garden has been erected on a massive scale, now operating as a living museum.

$\mathcal{D}$EVON

TAPELEY PARK

INSTOW, NEAR BIDEFORD, DEVON

The garden is off the A39, 2 miles to the north of Bideford.

This pink brick Georgian mansion has a 20th century Arts and Crafts Italian style garden, with terraces designed by John Belcher and later restored by Mary Keen and Carol Clein. The gardens overlook the River Torridge and have stunning views. There are now woodlands, a lake, an organic garden, an ornamental water garden, a shell house, icehouse and walled kitchen garden. The terraces are hedged with fuchsias and lavender, and there are fine clipped yews, an ilex tunnel, palms and other exotic plants.

BICTON GARDENS

EAST BUDLEIGH, BUDLEIGH SALTERTON, DEVON

The gardens are on the A376, 2 miles to the north of Budleigh Salterton.

These gardens extend to some 50 acres. The majority of the design dates to around 1874, but there is a palm house that was built in the early 1800s. There is no apparent evidence of the garden designer, although they are very much in the style of Bridgeman, Wise and London. There is an Italian garden, an oriental garden and a hermitage garden with a lake. There are several grass terraces, a parterre and a geometric basin.

KILLERTON HOUSE AND GARDEN

BROADCLYST, EXETER, DEVON

The garden is on the west side of the B3181, 7 miles to the northeast of Exeter.

The gardens surround an 18th century house and extend over a hillside, with particularly good views of Dartmoor. In essence this is a Victorian garden with various elements. There is a parterre, designed by William Robinson, a large rock garden set in an old quarry and an arboretum created by John Veitch. The Veitch family were the prime movers in gathering rare shrubs and trees from around the world. However, the garden is known primarily for its bulbs, azaleas, magnolias and herbaceous borders.

ROSEMOOR GARDEN

ROSEMOOR, TORRINGTON, DEVON

The garden is on the A3124 from Great Torrington, which is found after junction 27 of the M5.

The house at Rosemoor was originally a fishing lodge, owned by Lady Anne Berry. It was given to the Royal Horticultural Society in 1988. The site overlooks the Torridge Valley and extends to 40 acres. The gardens represent a cross-section of UK plants and trees, but there are also thriving plants from New Zealand and Australia. The garden exists largely as it was planned in the 1960s, although the plants and trees have matured. The emphasis is on species that enjoy warm and wet conditions.

DORSET

ATHELHAMPTON HOUSE GARDENS

ATHELHAMPTON, DORCHESTER, DORSET

The gardens are on the A35, 3 miles to the east of Dorchester.

An Arts and Crafts garden dating to around 1891 surrounds this 15th century manor house. Reginald Bloomfield designed the gardens with F. Inigo Thomas, and they were responsible for this formal style garden. Twelve yew pyramids dominate the Great Court, shown above. A terrace with two summer houses overlook the canal and a pool sits within a sunken garden. The garden has colour in all seasons. Spring sees snowdrops, summer roses and herbs, and in the autumn spectacular red vines snake the walls.

MAPPERTON GARDEN

BEAMINSTER, DORSET

The gardens are 2 miles to the southeast of Beaminster.

Although the gardens are in the Italian style and were laid out in the 1920s, the house is much older and is a Jacobean manor dating to around 1660. Mapperton is a set of valley gardens, reflecting three different periods of history. The upper level is Italian in style with grottos, stone ornaments and a fountain court. Next are 17th century fishponds and finally an orangery and lower garden with specimen trees and shrubs. Mapperton is surely one of the most enchanting gardens.

MINTERNE GARDEN

MINTERNE MAGNA, DORSET

The gardens are 9 miles to the north of Dorchester, on the A352.

The grounds at Minterne extend to some 20 acres within this 18th century serpentine park. It is set in a valley with lakes and a stream. The dominant features are the magnolias and rhododendrons, which tumble over small streams. Later in the year water lilies, eucryphias and hydrangeas appear. This woodland garden has a lower garden walk and an upland walk, all densely planted. It was once the home of Sir Winston Churchill and had been in his family since the early 1600s.

FORDE ABBEY GARDEN

NEAR CHARD, DORSET

The gardens are 4 miles to the south of Chard.

This 30 acre site was a former Cistercian monastery and after 1539 became a stately home. There are extensive herbaceous borders running alongside a canal, a rock garden designed by Jack Drake, a kitchen garden, a topiary enclosure, original monastic fishponds and a bog garden. Most of the garden was developed during the 1800s and is considered to be the best garden in the West Country. A carpet of crocuses covers 10 acres of the garden during February, eventually giving way to daffodils.

Somerset *and* Avon

GANTS MILL AND GARDEN

BRUTON, SOMERSET AND AVON

The gardens are half a mile to the southwest of Bruton, off the A359.

The historic watermill dates back to 1290 and there is a riverside walk that will take you to the top of the weir. The building now provides bed and breakfast accommodation and the gardens extend to just half an acre. Within the garden are ponds, waterfalls, rose and clematis arches, irises, oriental poppies, vegetables, dahlias and streams. The summer is dominated by delphiniums and poppies, which are replaced in early autumn by dahlias and rudbeckias.

GOLDNEY HALL

LOWER CLIFTON HILL, BRISTOL, SOMERSET AND AVON

The gardens are in the city of Bristol.

Goldney Hall was built in 1714 and is set in 10 acres of gardens. These contain no less than five follies, including a Gothic tower, ornamental canal, rotunda, and shell-lined grotto and mock bastion. The gardens were the pride and joy of Thomas Goldney and are on a hilltop position overlooking the Bristol. The grotto took 27 years to build, and the tower contained one of the earliest steam engines in the world.

HADSPEN GARDEN AND NURSERY

CASTLE CARY, SOMERSET AND AVON

The gardens are off the A371, 2 miles to the southeast of Castle Cary.

The gardens at Hadspen are in the Arts and Crafts tradition and are set around an old walled garden on a hillside. In 1987 Nori and Sandra Pope replanted the gardens and created extensive mixed borders using yellows, oranges, reds, plums, pinks and peaches. The nursery is renowned for its old-fashioned roses and herbaceous plants. Wildflowers are set in a meadow alongside the curved walled garden. Penelope Hobhouse began the restoration in 1960, but the Popes have extended and improved her initial designs.

HESTERCOMBE GARDENS

CHEDDON FITZPAINE, SOMERSET AND AVON

The gardens are 4 miles to the north of Taunton.

These gardens were designed just before the First World War, in a collaboration between Gertrude Jekyll and Edwin Lutyens. The house itself, now owned by Somerset County Council, is a Victorian villa. The gardens are set on three main levels. The planting and design includes Lutyen's seats, pergolas, pools, iris-fringed rills and steps. An 18th century Georgian garden has recently been restored, originally designed by Copleston Warre Bampfylde. In all, the gardens extend to 40 acres, incorporating temples, lakes and woodland walks.

$\mathscr{W}$ILTSHIRE

ABBEY HOUSE GARDEN

MALMESBURY, WILTSHIRE

The garden is 5 miles from junction 17 of the M4.

A Benedictine monastery was founded here in 666 and the monks cultivated medicinal herbs. The gardens now extend to some five acres. The current owners began work in 1994 with the idea to reproduce a garden reflecting its monastic use in growing fruit, herbs, vines and roses. The rose beds now have over 2,000 different varieties. A knot garden was added in 1999. The original monastic fishponds have been re-dug and ancient trees vie for attention with the camellias, hydrangeas and acers.

STOURHEAD GARDEN

NEAR WARMINSTER, WILTSHIRE

The gardens are 9 miles to the southwest of Warminster.

A wealthy English banker, heavily influenced by Italian art, inherited this estate in the 18th century. The gardens are inspired by the great landscape painters of the 17th century and include a temple and a grotto. The lake was dug in 1754, a five-arched bridge eight years later and a further temple in 1765. Most of the work can be attributed to Henry Hoare II. There are rhododendrons, azaleas and pelargoniums. The woods were under-planted by rhododendrons as early as 1791.

BOWOOD HOUSE
CLANE, WILTSHIRE

The gardens are 5 miles to the southeast of Chippenham.

This 18th century house stands in parkland designed by Capability Brown. There are sloping lawns stretching all the way to the lake far beyond. The gardens are essentially Italian in style and there is an encircling tree belt and serpentine lake. There is a cascade that was designed by Charles Hamilton and a Doric temple beside the lake. There is a separate 50 acre rhododendron walk, which is especially stunning during May and June. The house is the home of the Marquis and Marchioness of Landsdowne.

HEALE GARDEN
WOODFORD, SALISBURY, WILTSHIRE

The gardens are 4 miles to the north of Salisbury.

Harold Peto designed this 20th century Arts and Crafts garden in 1910, surrounding a 17th century house, which is sited on the bank of the River Avon. The owner at the time, Louis Greville, was a diplomat and brought over the Nikko Bridge (shown here) and teahouse from Japan. Although only eight acres, there is a huge selection of plants and shrubs, as well as roses, magnolia and acers. The water garden is particularly attractive, as are the clipped hedges and stonework.

WALES

Wales consists of some of the oldest and hardest rocks in Britain, many of them up to 700 million years old. It is a mountainous country and, indeed, a quarter of Wales is over 305 metres (1,000 feet). The Welsh coastline has estuaries and sandbanks and there is a huge contrast along the shoreline. However, none of these potential problems has dissuaded countless gardens from springing up and flourishing over the centuries.

One of the jewels in the crown of Wales, if not that of Britain, is the stunning Bodnant Garden in North Wales. It is a world apart. 18th century gardens surround Gothic houses and 18th century houses are complemented by 19th and 20th century designs. Even the country's sometimes-brutal past, exemplified in castles such as Chirk or Powis, have become tranquil oases. Chirk is now as famous for its pomegranates as it is for its towers and defensive walls.

There are two young gardens in the selection shown here. The four acre site at Veddw House and a similar size garden at The Dingle in Welshpool are no less stunning for their lack of history. Near Wrexham you will find not only Chirk Castle and its gardens designed by William Emes, but also his vision at Erddig, which now contains the National Collection of ivy.

BODNANT GARDEN

TAL-Y-CAFN, NEAR COLWYN BAY, CONWY, WALES

The garden is on the east side of the Conwy Valley, off the A470.

Beyond doubt, Bodnant is one of the finest gardens in the world. It overlooks the River Conwy and fans the slopes of the Snowdon range. Henry Duncton passed the garden to the National Trust in 1949. In effect, Bodnant has two parts: the upper part consisting of terraced gardens and informal lawns, and the lower containing the wild garden and pinetum. Spring sees masses of bulbs, fighting for attention with rhododendrons, magnolias, azaleas, camellias, laburnum arch and Chilean fire bush.

PLAS NEWYDD GARDEN
LLANFAIRPWLL, ANGLESEY, WALES

The gardens are on the A5, 2 miles west of Llanfairpwll.

The gardens surrounding this neo-Gothic house, designed by James Wyatt and dating to 1793, were suggested by plans made by Henry Repton. The gardens overlooking the Menai Straits and Snowdonia are essentially in a parkland style. Repton's eye for detail can be seen in most of the garden, but the terrace and rose garden were created in the 20th century. There is an Italianate garden with fountains and an arboretum with Australian plants. The parkland has many rhododendrons, azaleas and magnolias, particularly stunning in spring.

CHIRK CASTLE
CHIRK, WALES

The gardens are 5 miles to the south of Wrexham, off the A483.

Chirk Castle is a 14th century fortification, but is surrounded by a parkland dating from the 18th century and a garden from the 19th century. The gardens were created from a design made by William Emes with roses, herbaceous borders, clipped yews and a rock garden. The gardens are well known for their yew topiary and wonderful vistas. In the parkland there are many rhododendrons and azaleas, along with a lime walk. The castle and gardens offer fantastic views of the surrounding countryside.

ERDDIG GARDENS

NEAR WREXHAM, WALES

The gardens are off the A525, 2 miles to the southwest of Wrexham.

The house at Erddig was built between 1720 and 1740 and has a late 18th century park designed by William Emes. With the assistance of a bird's eye view of the garden drawn in 1739, the National Trust has been able to restore Erddig's gardens. They also used illustrations from the 19th and 20th centuries in order to create the Victorian garden and the parterre. Erddig has the National Collection of ivy, woodland walks, a canal, avenues and a walled garden.

POWIS CASTLE GARDEN

NEAR WELSHPOOL, WALES

The castle is a mile to the west of Welshpool.

Powis Castle dates back to the medieval period and its gardens, designed by William Winde, to the 17th century. Particularly stunning are the hanging terraces, which were built around 1680 and have been fully restored using an engraving dated 1742. The gardens are famous for their pomegranates, roses and collection of rare plants. The valley has been transformed over the years from a water garden to a landscaped park, then a kitchen garden and now a flower garden.

VEDDW HOUSE GARDEN

THE VEDDW, DEVAUDEN, WALES

The garden is 5 miles to the northwest of Chepstow, just off the B4293.

This house and gardens are located on the Welsh border. The gardens, which date back to the 1990s, contain a woodland garden, a meadow, a cotoneaster walk, magnolia walk, wild garden, a grey border and a fish garden. In all there are two acres of ornamental gardens and a further two acres of woodland areas. The grounds are most famous for their cornfield garden. There is also a reflecting pool, an ornamental vegetable plot, many roses and other themed gardens.

THE DINGLE

WELSHPOOL, POWYS, WALES

The gardens are off the A490, just outside of Welshpool.

The Dingle is a four acre garden run by Barbara and Roy Joseph. The gardens include woodland and a lakeside area and are designed to provide colour and interest throughout the year and to inspire gardeners. The planting is colour themed, with roses, herbaceous perennials, ornamental grasses, herbs, alpines, fruit trees and hedging plants. The adjoining nursery provides many of the plants for the garden. The garden is wonderfully secluded, with a network of paths and steps through the cultivated beds.

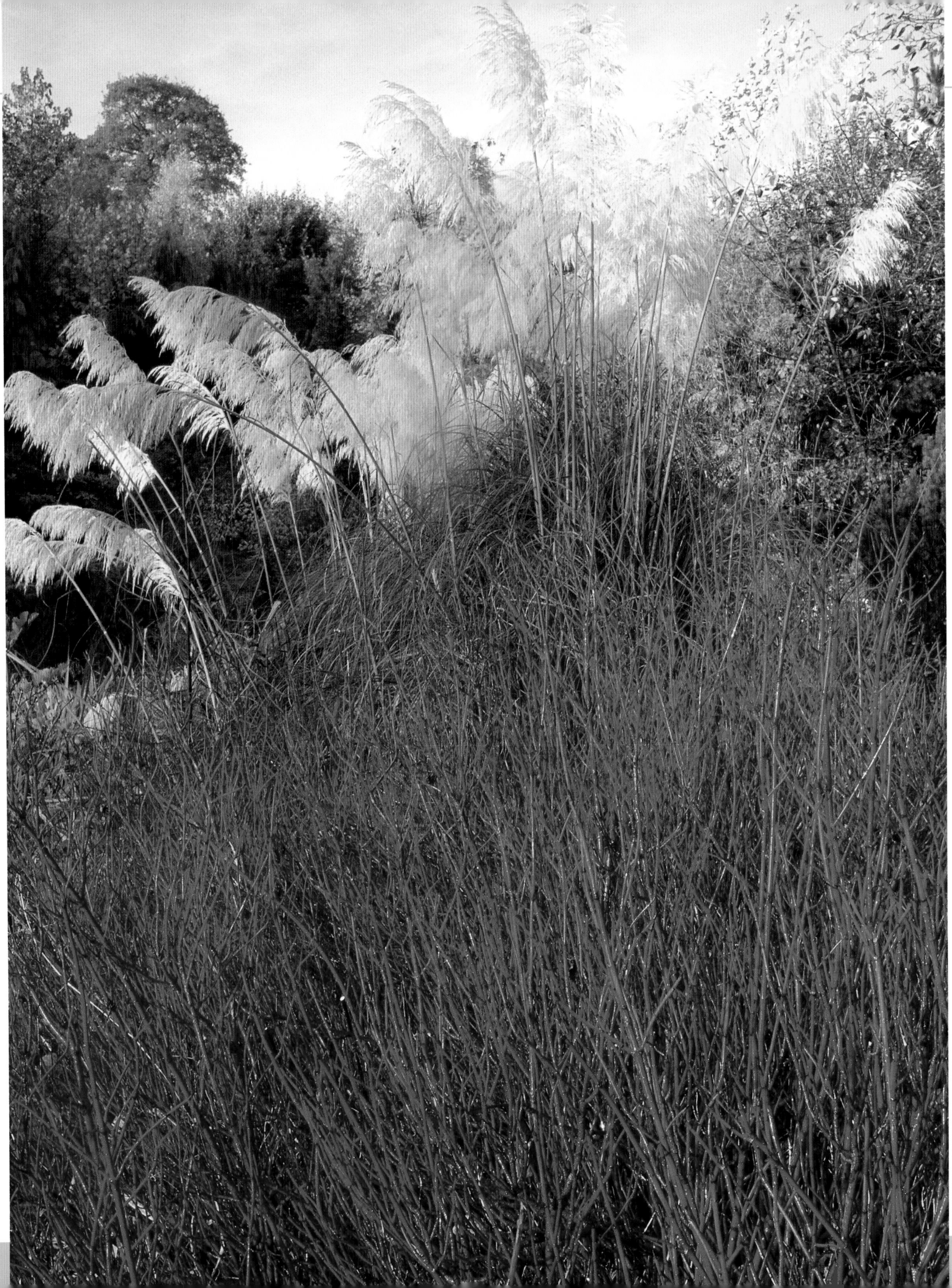

SCOTLAND

Scotland boasts some of the most beautiful and wild scenery in Britain, including the Highlands, the Midland Valley and the Southern Uplands. Whilst most of Scotland's industry is located in the middle part of the country, its gardens extend to the very reaches of the land.

It is something of a myth that Scotland suffers constantly from poorer and wetter weather. The Gulf Stream bathes the western seaboard and, as a result, some of the Highland gardens are the best in the country. The mild air takes the edge off the winter frosts and even tender plants can survive and thrive.

Scotland's rich, historical background provides the backdrop to some of the country's most stunning gardens. In Ayr, at Culzean Castle, you will find a 14th century fortification with 17th century gardens. At Kellie Castle there is a tower dating back to the 14th century and an Arts and Crafts garden designed by Robert Lorimer.

The great garden designers are no less apparent in Scotland than elsewhere in Britain, and neither is the variety and ingenuity shown. Tropical plants thrive in the heart of Edinburgh, while moorland near Inverness, based on black peat, boasts nearly 500 varieties of plants and trees.

DUNROBIN
CASTLE GARDENS
GOLSPIE, SUTHERLAND, SCOTLAND

The gardens are 50 miles to the north of Inverness.

In 1845, Sir Charles Barry, fresh from completing the Houses of Parliament, was employed by the Earl of Sutherland to remodel the castle believed to date back to 1235. Unfortunately the majority of the interior was destroyed in a fire in 1915. The gardens were also designed by Barry around 1850 and overlook the Moray Firth, incorporating terraces, ponds and fountains. The formal gardens, with their parterres, are heavily influenced by the gardens at Versailles. These give way to fine woodlands.

CULZEAN CASTLE
AND COUNTRY PARK
MAYBOLE, SCOTLAND

The gardens are 12 miles to the southwest of Ayr.

Robert Adam substantially rebuilt the castle around 1771. There is a 19th century terraced garden with a lily pond and borders. In all, the gardens extend to 560 acres, incorporating woodlands and coastal walks. There are wonderful wooded glades, concealed paths and stunning cliff-top views. One of the most impressive areas is the walled garden and the formal court garden, which is sunken into the landscape. The National Trust for Scotland now cares for the castle.

DRUMMOND CASTLE GARDENS

MUTHILL, NEAR CRIEFF, SCOTLAND

The gardens are off the A822, 2 miles to the south of Crieff.

The gardens around this ancient castle were first laid out at the beginning of the 17th century. They were substantially redesigned and then terraced in the early 19th century. There are ancient yew hedges and copper beech trees, which were planted by Queen Victoria in 1842. The majority of the planting and restoration took place in the 1950s. The gardens still retain a multiplex sundial dating from the 1630s and there is a large parterre in the shape of a St Andrew's cross.

CAWDOR CASTLE GARDEN

NAIRN, SCOTLAND

The garden is on the B9090, 5 miles to the southwest of Nairn.

This 14th century castle, with additions made in the 17th century, has three completely different gardens. The walled garden is the oldest. Probably constructed around 1620, it is now a thistle garden and holly maze. The flower garden dates to around 1700 and was designed as a late-summer and autumn garden, but has now been planted with bulbs, ornamental trees, shrubs and herbaceous borders. The final garden was constructed in the 1960s and is a wild garden, alongside Cawdor Burn.

LOGAN BOTANIC GARDEN

PORT LOGAN, NEAR STRANRAER, SCOTLAND

The gardens are off the B7065, 14 miles to the south of Stranraer.

Arguably, these gardens are one of the most exotic in the country, as they take full advantage of the warm air current from the Gulf Stream. The gardens are sub-tropical, with palms, tender plants and tree ferns. The walled garden has many colourful plants from the southern hemisphere and around the garden there are South African plants and even poppies from the Himalayas. The woodland garden, walled garden and terrace provide excellent views of the Galloway Hills and beyond.

ROYAL BOTANIC GARDEN

INVERLEITH ROW, EDINBURGH, SCOTLAND

The garden is 1.5 miles to the north of the city centre.

This 19th century garden boasts an arboretum and rock garden which were designed by Sir Isaac Bavley Balfour, dating to 1888. The gardens have the largest palm house in Britain, along with other glasshouses for temperate and tropical plants. The rock garden extends to two acres and has a stream, Chinese flowers, a water ravine and herbaceous borders. The garden is also renowned for its rhododendrons, orchids and alpines. The site provides wonderful panoramic views of the skyline of Edinburgh.

KELLIE CASTLE AND GARDEN

PITTENWEEM, SCOTLAND

The gardens are 8 miles to the south of St Andrews.

The castle was once the home of the Earls of Kellie and dates to around 1606, although there is an older tower dating to 1360. The castle was fully restored by the Lorimer family in 1878. There is a wonderful Arts and Crafts garden that was created by Robert Lorimer in 1880 for his parents. The National Trust for Scotland acquired the castle in 1970. The garden has many old-fashioned roses and herbaceous plants, all of which are organically cultivated.

INVEREWE GARDEN
POOLEWE, ROSS-SHIRE, SCOTLAND

The gardens are off the A832, 6 miles to the northeast of Gairloch.

In 1862 Osgood Mackenzie, the founder of Inverewe Garden, began the long task of transforming the heather moorland, a labour that lasted until he died in 1922. His daughter, Mairi Sawyer, passed the property over to the National Trust in 1952. The acidic black peat, barely two or three feet in depth, is now replete with 477 different varieties of plants and trees. The exposed peninsular is blessed with warm currents of air from the Gulf Stream, a major factor in its success.

CRATHES CASTLE GARDEN
BANCHORY, SCOTLAND

The gardens are on the A93, 15 miles to the west of Aberdeen.

This four acre garden dates back to the late 1500s, although the majority of the garden now appears to be in the Arts and Crafts tradition. The castle is 16th century. In the 20th century Sir James Burnett designed the garden, including a walled area and sculptured topiary. There are eight distinctive gardens, and a large greenhouse contains the National Collection of malmaison carnations. Of particular interest are the double herbaceous borders, the Red Garden, the Golden Garden and the June borders.

INDEX

PICTURE CREDITS

With grateful thanks to:

Photographs by Andy Williams ©: 1, 3, 4l, 6, 9bl, 12-13, 24, 32, 34-35, 36, 38-39, 50-51, 54-55, 62, 63, 68, 72, 77, 78-79, 82-83, 84, 85, 86, 87, 92-93, 94, 96-97, 100, 101, 102, 106, 107, 108-109, 110, 113, 114-115, 122, 124, 125, 128, 129, 130, 131, 132, 133, 134, 136, 137, 138, 139, 140, 141, 142-143, 144, 145, 146, 147, 148, 149, 150, 151, 154, 155, 160, 161, 164, 172, 173, 174, 178, 180, 188, 189, 190, 191

Garden Picture Library ©: David Askham: 197; Pernilla Bergdahl: 5, 159; Richard Bloom: 120-121; Mark Bolton: 163, 167, 169, 170; Clive Boursnell: 25, 49, 58, 80, 116; Rex Butcher: 158; Brian Carter: 162; Bob Challinor: 175; Kathy Charlton: 195; Eric Crichton: 8, 182; David Dixon: 61, 66-67, 156-157; John Ferro Sims: 9tr, 192-193; Nigel Francis: 42; Christopher Gallagher: 7tl, 29, 56, 90, 95; Suzie Gibbons: 112; John Glover: 46-47, 48, 81, 119, 184, 185; Nick Holmes: 65; Anne Hyde: 166; Jason Ingram: 165, 168; Lamontagne: 4r, 76; Gerard Liston: 75; Marianne Majerus: 64; Nick Meers: 15, 16-17; Clive Nichols: 30, 103; Jerry Pavia: 194; Cressida Pemberton-Pigott: 19; Clay Perry: 28, 37, 45, 60, 69, 74, 117, 171, 183, 200; Kevin J Richardson: 181; John Riley: 73, 99; Vivian Russell: 14, 18; Alec Scaresbrook: 88; JS Sira: 98, 111, 118, 123, 126-127; Juliette Wade: 59; Steven Wooster: 196

The Berkeley and Spetchley Estates: 89

Fred Cholmeley: 44

Cobble Hey Farm & Gardens: 20

Doddington Hall Gardens, Lincoln: 43

Lamport Hall & Gardens, Northampton: 57

Leicestershire County Council: 53

Arabella Lennox-Boyd: 22-23

Longframlington Gardens: 31

Raby Estates, Raby Castle: 33

David Roberts: 21

Sabina Rüber: 91

Whatton Estate, Whatton Gardens: 7br, 52